Oregon Outlaws

Tales of Old-Time Desperadoes

OREGON OUTLAWS

TALES OF OLD-TIME DESPERADOES

by
Gary & Gloria Meier

First Edition, July 1996

10 9 8 7 6 5 4 3 2

ISBN: 1–886609–05–5

All photos by authors unless otherwise noted.

PUBLISHED BY:
Tamarack Books, Inc.
PO Box 190313
Boise, ID 83719-0313

Printed in the United States of America

To Dick Lofton and Steve Tindall,
who should have been lawmen in the last century.

When bad boys steal horses and mules,
Auburn lets them hang around for awhile.
Sheriff George Washington Hall
Baker County, Oregon, 1862

TABLE OF CONTENTS

ACKNOWLEDGMENTS

NO BOOK REQUIRING historical research can be possible without the help of many persons. We would like to thank the following people and organizations for their generous and considerate efforts: Bob Chandler, Wells Fargo Bank History Department; Will Harmon, Special Collections, University of Oregon Library; Michael McQuade, Oregon State Archives; Bob Wise; Baker County Historical Society; Bowman Museum, Prineville, Oregon; Douglas County Museum; Eastern Oregon Museum; Grant County Historical Museum; Harney County Historical Society; Josephine County Historical Society; Lane County Historical Museum; Marion County Historical Society; Oregon Historical Society; Portland Police Museum; Southern Oregon Historical Society; Union County Museum; Wallowa County Historical Society.

We are especially grateful to our friend Bill Hawley, former historian of the Oregon State Sheriffs' Association, who took countless hours away from his other projects to answer questions, dig out data and photos from his voluminous files, and provide Oregon lawmen and outlaw artifacts for us to photograph.

To all of these, our heartfelt thanks. This is your book as much as it is ours.

The Authors

AUTHORS' FOREWORD

THE COLORFUL HISTORY of Oregon is the sum of many lives, from ancient Indian cultures to trail blazers to ox-team pioneers to empire builders. Most of these were hardworking, law-abiding men and women of vision, endurance, and accomplishments, who carved from the frontier a new state rich with promises that have been fulfilled.

But blended with the times of Oregon's past were individuals of a different sort. They were a reckless breed, who scoffed at all law or made their own. In their wake were left such Oregon place names as Murder Creek, Bandit Springs, Rustler Peak, and Thief Valley. Records of their nefarious deeds—gunfights, murders, rustling, and stagecoach, train, and bank robberies—form a part of Oregon's history. The players in these dramas are interesting to us today, and, filtered through the softening lens of time, some of them have even become picturesque.

With a few notable exceptions, these accounts of Oregon's badmen are not commonly known. Their escapades lie buried in musty newspapers and forgotten court records and writings of long gone old-timers. Yet many of these true tales rival those told of Jesse James, the

Daltons, Butch Cassidy, and others of the West's better-known banditti.

The stories of Oregon's outlaws are also the stories of the lawmen who pursued them. Occasionally, a courageous lawman was killed by his quarry, and some of those accounts are here, too.

Finally, this volume is not intended as a complete chronicle of lawlessness in Oregon. It is an attempt to offer the curious reader, through a selection of carefully researched occurrences, a new perspective on the history of our nation's thirty-third state—the outlaws of Oregon.

Gary & Gloria Meier
Eugene, Oregon

CHAPTER 1

Lawlessness in the Early Years

Outlawry was rare during the earliest exploration and pioneer years in Oregon. Though there were a few thieves, gamblers, and idlers among the first adventurers and settlers, major criminal acts were infrequent. The scant population was scattered, and there was little or nothing to steal; if something was stolen, there was no ready way by which the culprit could escape into another district or community.

Though Oregon had been too young for much lawlessness before the 1850s, the growing population—13,000 in 1850 to 52,000 by 1860—and the discovery of gold brought guns and greed to the green frontier. Thieves, highwaymen, and gamblers, lured by easy wealth to the new towns and mining camps, preyed on miners, businessmen, and travelers. Later came horse and cattle rustlers, and others with evil intent who flocked to the saloons and gambling joints that mushroomed through the settled places in Oregon.

Among the early free-roaming outlaws who left bodies in their trails as they followed the lure of someone else's gold were Matt Bledsoe, Boone Helm, Ferd Patterson, and Spanish Tom.

Matt Bledsoe: Born For a Rope

Where Madison "Matt" Bledsoe came from originally is not known, but after two killings in the upper Sacramento Valley, he stormed into Oregon in 1861 as a twenty-one-year-old outlaw. Matt hung around the Eugene City area for a while, and in the summer of 1861 he killed again.

Willamette Street in Eugene City, where Matt Bledsoe killed Hugh Feeney in 1861. *(Authors' collection)*

It happened on Willamette, the town's dusty main street. Hugh Feeney was an elderly man who somehow got on the wrong side of Bledsoe, and Matt caved in his head with a rock. The murder created considerable excitement in the little river town, but Bledsoe escaped to Idaho. Shortly after arriving in the Florence mining district, he killed a man on Whitebird Creek.

Returning eventually to Oregon, Matt settled for a

while at the wild, booming gold camp of Auburn in the Blue Mountains. He became the leader of the criminal element in Auburn and was a leading denizen in gambling dens and brothels.

In the fall of 1862, a fatal poisoning of a miner by Matt's partner, French Pete, caused a local commotion. French Pete was arrested by Sheriff George Washington Hall, tried quickly by Judge Sidney Abell, and hanged. Matt Bledsoe stayed in Auburn only a short while after the Frenchman was strung up. The deciding factor in Matt's decision to shake the dust of Auburn from his boots came two months later when a lynch mob killed another Bledsoe crony. That was too much for Matt; between the sheriff and lynch mobs, Auburn was no longer safe for the man who had earlier vowed that he would "as soon kill a man as eat breakfast."

Bledsoe's next Oregon foray landed him in prison. Late on a cold October night in 1864, Matt was en route to a Portland saloon with Charley Cavin and two of the city's "soiled doves." At the corner of First and Morrison Streets, Matt and Charley became embroiled in a controversy over claims on the two ladies. The heated words came to a swift conclusion when Matt smashed Charley on the head with the butt of a gun. Charley dropped, and with two more blows of the gun, Matt killed him.

On this occasion Bledsoe did not escape the firm grasp of the law as he had in times past. He was immediately arrested, tried, and convicted of second-degree murder. He was sentenced on December 20, 1864 to the penitentiary, then located in Portland, to serve out a life term. He was twenty-four years old. But the outside world had not seen the last of Matt Bledsoe.

In May 1866, the convicts at the Portland prison were transferred in chains to the new facility at Salem. On

Matt Bledsoe killed Charley Cavin over a Portland red-light girl at First and Morrison Streets. *(Authors' collection)*

August 27 of that year Matt took leave of the prison in dramatic style. The escape was detailed in the September 3, 1866 Salem *Oregon Statesman:*

> In the afternoon of Monday last Bledsoe, one of the convicts and a notorious desperado, called upon Mr. Allard, the warden, for some medicine. The warden, upon entering the office to obtain it, was suddenly seized by Bledsoe; wrenching himself loose he then sprang for the door where he was met and seized by four or five other convicts who had armed themselves with knives from the kitchen. About the same time Mr. Shaw, the superintendent, was seized by two of the convicts at the blacksmith shop and forced to go quietly along with them, assuring him that no harm should be done if he did so. On turning around, Mr. Shaw saw the warden being forced toward him, bleeding at the mouth.
>
> At this juncture Bledsoe, leaving the warden, came to

> Mr. Shaw and being armed with a butcher knife threatened him with death if he made any disturbance; to which the superintendent replied that he should do his duty at any peril.
>
> Here Mr. Alden, foreman of the brickyard, was brought up, he having also been captured, and the whole party was forced along toward the east end of the new building where there was an opening in the fence.
>
> When they had passed the end of the building, Messrs. Barry and Hurley, two guards who were stationed on the platform of the fence, came opposite to them and within thirty or forty feet.
>
> The superintendent ordered the guards to fire, but they seeing the dangers to the officers, did not comply. The party soon reached the opening of the fence where several guards were stationed. As the temporary fence was reached, Mr. Shaw clenched his arm around one of the pieces of which it was composed, causing a halt among those who held him. Allard and Alden were forced through the passage. When the convicts, noticing their exposed position, began a retreat, Bledsoe and Wright fled for the brush.
>
> The guards opened fire and Wright was brought down while Bledsoe escaped with a wound in the left shoulder. The main body retreated within the enclosure and soon made another rush for the fence where eight more escaped and several more were turned back even though they were beyond the fence.

Matt was a free man for exactly forty days. He was recaptured on October 5, 1866 and returned to the Salem prison. He served six more years of his "life" sentence, then was released on Christmas Day 1872. Life's lessons were apparently difficult for him to absorb, for he moved to the Arizona Territory, where he was soon hanged for another murder.

Boone Helm: "Hideous Monster of Depravity"

Boone Helm was an outlaw from cradle to grave. He had the distinction of never working at an honest job in his life of forty-plus years. He was born sometime in the 1820s in Kentucky, grew up mean, and by his early twenties was an accomplished horse thief and robber. In 1851 Boone murdered his first man, a friend named Littlebury Shoot, whom he stabbed to death in Missouri. After the killing, Boone rode hell-bent out of the district, but was soon captured. He broke out of jail and headed for California, where he drifted around the gold country and San Francisco. Helm researchers claim he killed at least three men while in California, and possibly as many as twelve.

Oregon was host to this unwelcome visitor on a number of occasions in his career of lawlessness. He first showed up in the spring of 1858 at The Dalles, at that time called Dalles City, and it was wide-open and wild. Horse thieves, gamblers, fugitives, and other ill-mannered folk elbowed one another on the town's only street. Shootings and stabbings were almost daily occurrences, and Boone Helm fit right in. Through the spring, summer, and fall of 1858, Boone became a leader of the lawless element preying on the local garrison soldiers and the immigrants passing through on the Columbia River.

While in Dalles City, Boone acquired an Indian wife. Once he was thrown in jail on a minor charge and promptly escaped by digging out with tools brought by his wife. Fearing recapture and extradition to California for murder, Helm left Dalles City in October 1858 with a party of gamblers headed to Utah. When the group reached the Grande Ronde Valley, near present La Grande, Boone suggested and planned a large-scale theft of Indian horses, which the white men would share and sell in Salt Lake City.

The raid did not come off due to a dissenting member of the party who warned the Indians to guard their herd.

Boone Helm went on to Utah and made his way back to California, where he engaged in horse rustling and more killing. Near Lodi he shot a man in the head and soon after boarded a ship, returning once more to Oregon. In Portland and The Dalles he quickly drifted back into a life of roadside robbery and murder. It was during this period, 1859–1860, that Boone killed several more men in eastern Oregon, according to a later Portland *Oregonian* item, though the details of those deaths are now lost.

In the spring of '62, Helm murdered a man in Idaho called "Dutch Fred." Leaving with great haste for Canada, Boone and a pal, Brocky Jack, killed a man later that summer on the trail from the Cariboo mines in British Columbia. Helm followed that killing with three more in the same area. The bloody-handed outlaw was captured in the fall of 1862 on the Fraser River. He broke jail, but was immediately caught. He escaped again and fled back to Washington.

Boone was arrested in January 1863 at Olympia by Sheriff Moxlie on a charge of disorderly conduct. According to the January 22, 1863 *Oregonian,* Helm "had been swaggering about town for some days, swearing that he would kill a man before he left town. He was armed with two revolvers and a huge knife."

It was learned that he was wanted for murder in Florence, Idaho, but before he could be sent there he broke jail in Olympia, stole a horse, and headed again for Canada. He was caught at Yale on the Fraser River, and without delay was taken south to Port Townsend, Washington Territory, by that city's marshal, who happened to be in Yale. Helm dug out of the Port Townsend jail, but was recaptured and taken to Florence for trial.

Surprisingly, the result of the Idaho trial in the spring of 1863 was an acquittal for Helm due to a lack of evidence. Temporarily a free man because California, Canada, and Oregon had not notified the Idaho authorities that he was wanted, Boone stayed around Boise City for awhile, then went to southern Oregon.

A settler in Oregon's Rogue River Valley took Boone Helm in for several weeks, not realizing the inclination his guest had for killing. Soon after Helm took leave of his kindly host, the farmer received word from a woman in Yreka that Boone and two others were planning to return to the settler's homestead, kill him, and steal his large herd of cattle. Thus warned, the stalwart farmer waited, well-armed, for the outlaw to arrive. When Boone rode up ahead of the others, the settler disarmed him at gunpoint and held him captive overnight. The next morning he released Helm, but threatened to use his shotgun if the outlaw ever returned.

Unwilling to tangle further with the farmer, and no doubt concerned about the notoriety his aborted raid would bring, Boone scooted back to Idaho in the late summer of 1863. He drifted on to Virginia City, a newly established gold camp, then in Idaho Territory (now in Montana). There he joined the infamous Sheriff Henry Plummer's gang of cutthroat road agents. Murders and robberies continued to be Boone's way of life until he was hanged with other members of the gang by Virginia City vigilantes on January 14, 1864.

Game and cool to the end, according to witnesses, Boone was placed on a wooden box and the noose was fitted around his neck. Taking a final look through what one vigilante called "fiery eyes," the Kentuckian yelled: "Every man for his principles! Hurrah for Jeff Davis! Let her rip!" The box was knocked away and Boone Helm's killing days were over.

A vigilante leader, Thomas Dimsdale, called Boone Helm a "savage and defiant marauder," and "a wild and reckless character." Another vigilante, Nathaniel Langford, said Helm was "one of those hideous monsters of depravity whom neither precept nor example could have saved from a life of crime." It was good riddance—the people of Oregon and the Northwest sighed in relief.

Ferd Patterson: The Silk Vest Gunfighter

Another of the early badmen who plied their trade in Oregon was a dapper fellow named J. Ferdinand Patterson. That he was a killer there is no doubt, but with the exception of two incidents, his known disagreements ended in more or less sporting gunfights in true Western style—that is, he let the other guy go for a gun before he killed him. Oregon was witness to some of that gunplay.

Most of Ferd Patterson's early life is lost to historical records, though it is known that he was a native of Tennessee. He was born in 1821 and spent much of his boyhood in Texas, where he fell in early with some of the desperate and bloody men of the border country. He struck California in 1850 at the height of the gold rush, where gambling was his chief occupation.

Ferd was of solid build, over six feet tall, with blue eyes and light hair streaked with gray. He sometimes sported sandy side-whiskers and a thick, curving mustache. His clothes ran to the usual attire of his profession: long black coat, plaid trousers, red, white, or black silk vest, and black wide-brimmed hat. Across his vest he habitually wore a long watch chain made of California nuggets.

Patterson always went armed and his favorite weapons were an ivory-handled Colt .31-caliber Baby Dragoon

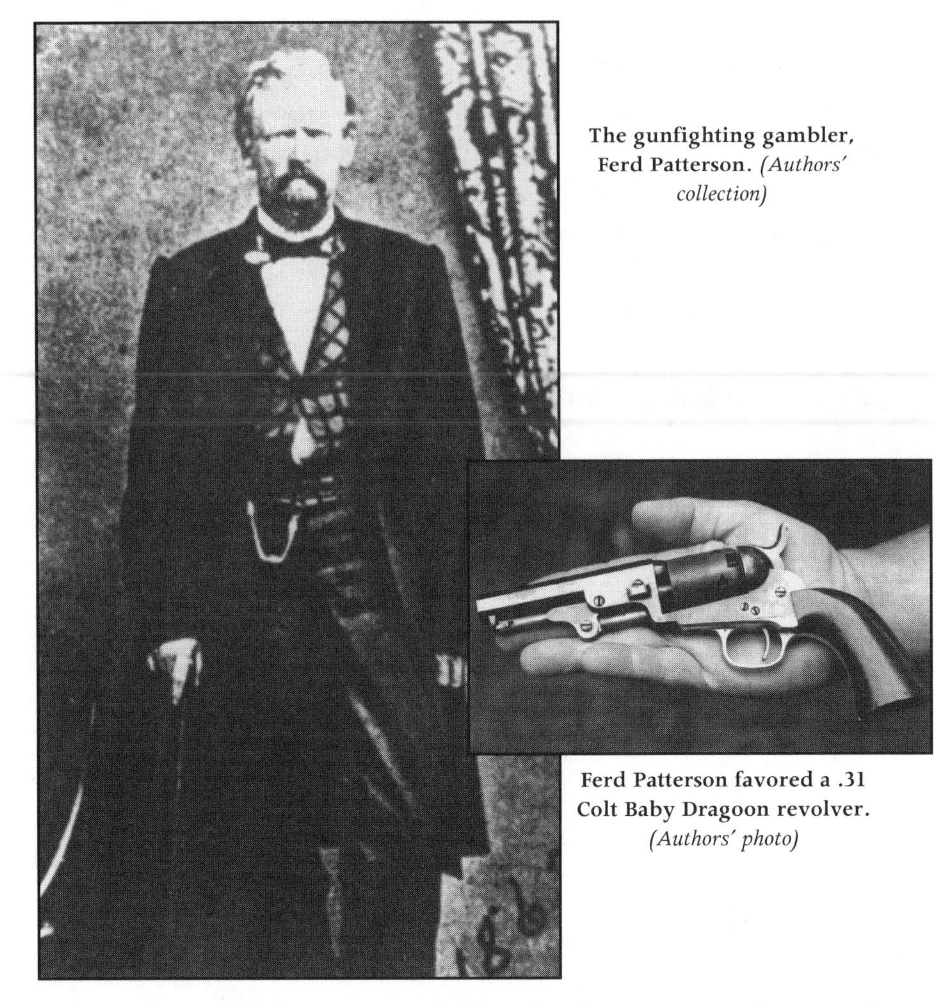

The gunfighting gambler, Ferd Patterson. *(Authors' collection)*

Ferd Patterson favored a .31 Colt Baby Dragoon revolver. *(Authors' photo)*

revolver and a matching bowie knife. He was adept with both and had achieved a reputation for their use in California long before leaving for Oregon.

Whiskey was Ferd Patterson's chief weakness. Sober, he was often affable and usually somewhat reasonable. But fired with the devils of spirituous beverage—a frequent state for him—he became touchy, mean-tongued, and very dangerous. He was known to have engaged in a number of street fights with gun and knife during his early years in the Sierra gold camps and San Francisco, and in 1856 he was shot while coming out of a saloon in Yreka. Not seriously injured, he recovered to engage in several more scrapes in northern California.

In 1859, Patterson wandered over the Siskiyou Mountains to the gold country of southern Oregon. He was in a number of fights in Jacksonville, but the one that almost ended his violent career took place that same year in the nearby gold camp of Waldo. For months Ferd was a familiar figure in the gambling saloons of the district, and he was doing well at his trade, mining the miners. But somehow he became embroiled in an ongoing dispute with George Wells, the Waldo precinct constable.

Wells was a scrappy former Texas Ranger who operated a small saloon on the main street, and he was not a man to fool with, for George carried a big .44 Walker Colt, a holdover from his Ranger days. The gun was a hand-cannon with a nine-inch barrel and a loaded weight of four-and-a-half pounds. Also, when he was going about his law duties in the rowdy gold camp, Wells sheathed his left arm in thick leather from elbow to wrist to guard against knife thrusts.

The reasons for the trouble between Ferd and Wells are not recorded, but one day in 1859 it exploded in front of Wells' saloon. Hot words led to threats, and suddenly both men were dodging and shooting. Patterson was badly hit in the side, a heavy half-ounce slug from Wells' gun destroying two of his ribs on the way in. One of Patterson's shots struck Wells in an arm, shattering a bone. Both men fell to the ground and Patterson, believing the wound in his side was fatal, emptied his gun at Wells, but none of the bullets took effect.

George Wells soon recovered, though his arm was crippled for life. For some time it was thought that Ferd Patterson would die from his wound. After a lengthy recuperation, however, he was on his feet again, seemingly not at all changed by his closeness to death, though there is no record that he took any further action toward George Wells.

Ferd moved back to California in 1860. In Sacramento that year he had another gunfight and was again shot, this time not seriously.

In the fall of 1861, Patterson left San Francisco and headed north to Portland, Oregon. One night he was drinking in the Bank Exchange Saloon with a character called "One-Armed Brown." George Staples, a steamer captain, was also in the saloon with some friends. Staples, a staunch and well-known Unionist, lifted his glass and loudly announced: "Here's to the Union." Ferd Patterson, a native Southerner and Confederate sympathizer, replied equally as loud: "To hell with the Union!" There was a heated exchange of words between them, but after throwing some bar glasses, Ferd withdrew.

Later that night all the participants in the affray wound up in the Pioneer Hotel at Front and Washington Streets, where threats between Patterson and Staples were renewed. Suddenly, the Unionists in the crowd rushed at the gambler, and Ferd ran up the stairs to the second floor landing. Staples went after him, but when the captain reached the top of the stairs, Patterson gunned him down.

Ferd fled from the hotel and surrendered to a deputy sheriff before Staples' friends could avenge his death. As the officer was taking Patterson to jail, a mob of Unionists friendly to Captain Staples appeared and threatened to lynch his killer. About this time Sheriff Addison M. Starr arrived and, with drawn gun, announced that he would kill the first person to touch Patterson. The mob slowly dispersed and Ferd was locked in jail.

The next day he was released on a heavy bond furnished by soon-to-be U.S. Senator Benjamin Stark, a loyal secessionist, and two prominent Portland businessmen. Patterson was tried and acquitted of murder when the pro-Confederate jury decided he had acted in self-defense.

Some time after the Staples killing, Ferd Patterson was again brought to the attention of the public by a knife attack on a woman. He was arrested for the act, but was released on a $500 bond to await trial. He remained in Portland only long enough to pack his valise, then headed straight up the Columbia River toward Idaho.

In Idaho City Patterson made his name known by public fights and boisterous conduct, and was arrested several times by Sheriff Sumner Pinkham. Patterson and Pinkham had several nasty altercations, and on July 23, 1865 they ran into each other on a hotel veranda. After hot words were exchanged, both men reached for their guns. Ferd was quicker on the draw and drilled Sumner Pinkham twice, killing him.

A trial was held and Ferd was acquitted by what the papers indicated was a "friendly" (Southern) jury. Immediately upon his release he went to Walla Walla, where he soon came to the attention of the local vigilante committee.

On a Thursday morning in February 1866, Ferd visited the barber shop of Richard Bogle, where he removed his coat and gunbelt and hung them on a wall peg, then sat back in the chair for a relaxing shave. A night watchman named Thomas Donahue, who had connections with the vigilante committee, came in and walked into the back room of Bogle's shop.

After the barber finished Ferd's shave, the gunman sat up in the chair to have his hair combed. Suddenly, Donahue appeared with a pistol and shot Ferd in the face, the bullet passing through his cheek. The wounded gambler leaped from the chair and went running from the shop, evidently in too much shock to retrieve his gun from the wall peg.

Outside the barber shop, Donahue shot Ferd once in the throat and once in the back. Patterson stumbled into Welch's Saloon next door and collapsed on the floor. Donahue approached and fired twice more into the dying gunman. The night watchman was arrested and jailed, but the trial somehow resulted in a hung jury. He was not re-tried.

Today in a Walla Walla cemetery one can find a small headstone with this inscription:

J.F. PATTERSON
ASSASSINATED
FEB. 15, 1866
AGED 45 YEARS

"Spanish Tom," A Powder River Desperado

History knows him only as "Spanish Tom." He had a name and a past, but they have been clouded by a time when few records were kept and a drifter brought nothing with him except a gun, a bedroll, and a horse—sometimes all stolen. The one thing Spanish Tom did leave in the record was an accurate account of his dramatic death.

He appeared in eastern Oregon with the gold rush of 1861, and when Auburn was established as a rip-roaring boomtown, Spanish Tom was there. He was a gambler, a horse thief from Powder River, Oregon, and a criminal associate of Matt Bledsoe.

On a day in late November 1862, two miners, John Desmond and William Lybia, were playing poker in an Auburn saloon. Spanish Tom joined the game, but a dispute soon arose over money and abusive words spewed back and forth. The miners then left the table to put an end to the quarrel. Not satisfied with the outcome, Tom followed. Outside, he drew a knife and attacked them, killing both instantly. Then he ran directly to his horse and galloped out of town.

Sheriff George Washington Hall, Baker County, Oregon.
(Oregon State Sheriffs' Association)

Though there were a number of witnesses to the double murder, there was a delay in notifying Sheriff George Hall. When he learned of the killings, Hall formed a posse and rode in pursuit of Spanish Tom. After an intense two-day search, the killer was run to ground at Mormon Basin and brought back to Auburn, where he was placed in a guarded room.

Now things began to get dicey for the Spaniard. The room chosen as a makeshift jail was a storeroom attached to a saloon, for Baker County was newly formed and no courthouse or jail had yet been built. The small room, closely watched by Hall's armed men, was the center of attention through the night by a multitude of miners who brazenly voiced the opinion that Tom should decorate the limb of a tree forthwith.

The next morning, the prisoner was brought into the "courtroom," with one ankle still attached to a long chain that had been used to secure him overnight. The chain dragged on the rough wooden floor behind Tom as he was escorted into court and placed in a chair. Sheriff Hall deputized forty men, who observed the proceedings inside and outside the saloon with wary eyes and ready rifles.

Judge Sidney Abell took his place at the head of the room and prepared to conduct a preliminary hearing. But he was soon interrupted by a delegation of miners who demanded the examination be conducted outside where all could see and hear. The throng around the saloon was dense, hundreds of miners having left their claims to be certain justice was done.

Sheriff Hall and Judge Abell decided to comply with the miners' demand in order to keep peace and allow the proceedings to commence without further interruption. Besides, though the huge mob was in an ugly mood, this was a brand-new county with law and authority and a sense of doing things right. And, of course, there were the forty rifles.

The site chosen as an open-air court was on a hillside west of town, and reports of the day indicate the mob was 2,000 strong. Even accounting for exaggeration, the crowd far outnumbered the guards. On the long walk to the hillside court, there were shouts demanding that the prisoner be surrendered and lynched. Sheriff Hall and Justice Abell, though, were determined that "Judge Lynch" would not rule the day. They made their way to the hill with the prisoner, who, according to contemporary accounts, stayed cool and outwardly calm through the ordeal.

Judge Abell took a position behind his judicial bench, a large flat rock, and opened court. Just how far he was able to proceed with the examination is difficult to determine because the reports differ. Some say he swore in and took testimony from a number of witnesses; others say he had not really begun. But all agreed on one significant point: at some moment in the proceedings the huge throng of mad miners grabbed the prisoner.

Hall could not regain control as the vigilante miners surged on Spanish Tom, took hold of the chain still attached to his ankle, and began to run down the hill toward town with the hapless killer sliding along on the ground behind. Reaching the main street, the frenzied miners looped a rope around Tom's neck and ran madly down the street, dragging him in the dust to the far edge of town. Along the way his head hit a log. By the time they reached the chosen tree, they were cheated out of their intended purpose, for Tom had already bid adieu to the turmoil of this life. They hoisted him anyway.

That was the end of Spanish Tom, the Powder River desperado. Judge Abell's official record of the affair reported the result this way:

The People of the State of Oregon (
vs (Murder
Spanish Tom (

Complaint filed the 21st day of November, 1862. Warrant issued of same date. The defendant brought into court the 22nd day of November, 1862. Kelly appointed for prosecution and McLaughlin for defendant. Witnesses sworn and testified—mob seized the defendant —Dragged him through the street and hung his lifeless body on a tree.

S. Abell
Justice of the Peace

CHAPTER 2

STAGECOACHES WERE EASY PICKINGS

IN THE EARLY 1860S, stagecoaches became the chief means of transporting passengers, mail, and express overland through Oregon. For the outlaw, the lure of the stagecoach was the gold it carried. Express companies such as Wells Fargo contracted with the various stage companies to carry regular express shipments—commonly gold coin, dust, and bullion—to and from Oregon's commerce centers.

Until railroads replaced stagecoaches, a tremendous amount of gold was carried in locked wooden boxes and leather pouches under the stage drivers' feet. An item in The Dalles *Mountaineer* on June 15, 1866, reported that nearly $200,000 in gold (over $4,500,000 in today's value) had come through town in one week from the mines to the east. In addition to the express shipments, money and gold dust was also sent by registered mail on the stagecoaches.

The huge amount of treasure moving through Oregon resulted in countless "roadside withdrawals" by masked bandits. Newspapers of the day carried frequent, sometimes daily, items announcing stage robberies by road agents. Nowhere in Oregon were coaches safe from these brigands, who took a cue in one way or another from their earlier English brother Dick Turpin's cry: "Stand and deliver!" The lure of quick wealth was too great, the robbing of a stage too easy.

Here are some true tales of stage robbery in the Oregon style.

ROAD AGENTS IN THE SISKIYOUS

Daily stagecoach service between Sacramento and Portland began on September 15, 1860. The California Stage Company's 710-mile route linked the two Pacific Coast states with a long-awaited overland means of transporting people, mail, and gold. It was not easy staging. At the center of the route, along the California-Oregon border, was a massive barrier which proved the most hazardous stretch on the entire road: the formidable Siskiyou Mountains. The narrow road wound up and through this maze of peaks and gorges, along sheer cliffs and grades so steep that six-horse teams were needed to pull the coaches over the top.

Lawmen and settlements were scarce in the Siskiyou district. Cole's Stage Station was at the southern foot of the mountains in California, and Barron's Stage Station was on the north side in Oregon. Near the summit was the Siskiyou Toll House. Those three small clusters of buildings and people were the only places of relative safety in the mountains. Past these brief stopping points two daily stagecoaches—one northbound, one southbound—carried an abundance of wealth into the wilds of the Siskiyou.

The lure of easy riches in a rugged and sparsely populated region drew a parade of road agents, including the storied Black Bart. Stage holdups came to be an expected, frustrating, and dangerous fact of life, and the gruff command to "Throw down the box and be damned quick," was often heard on the Siskiyou grades.

The accumulated loss to stage robberies was an expensive proposition for Wells Fargo & Company, whose records show that shipments of from $5,000 to $10,000 in gold were not uncommon. Company policy provided for the full and immediate payment to any customer who suffered a loss by robbery of an express box, and to its great credit, Wells Fargo & Company could say with all honesty that not one person ever lost a dollar in money or property entrusted to its care.

Aided by local sheriffs, Wells Fargo detectives worked long days, weeks, and months attempting to keep pace with the rising tide of robberies. They offered and paid rewards, followed tips and leads, and became intimately acquainted with the rough Siskiyou country. And they caught stage robbers.

But the pickings were good, and the robberies continued. During some months not a week went by without a holdup. In the first week of June 1876 three stage robberies prompted Deputy Sheriff John Halleck to say in the Jacksonville *Democratic Times* what everyone already knew, "The Siskiyou Mountains is a rough country to hunt a thief, as you might get within ten feet of him and not see him owing to the dense thicket of chaparral."

The second week of November, the same year, was another triple robbery week. Ben Holladay, the Southwest stagecoach king, was a passenger on one of the coaches that was stopped while he was en route to San Francisco from Portland with his wife and sister. Holladay later told the *Yreka Journal* that "looking down the barrels of a shotgun with a masked individual at the breech gives a man a peculiar feeling, not enjoyable."

After the fourth robbery in two weeks, the editor of

the *Ashland Tidings* declared on June 1, 1877, "Stage robberies are certainly frequent along the Oregon and California line. A company of vigilantes would not be a bad thing whenever one of the desperadoes is caught."

The Roseburg *Douglas Independent,* at the close of an article reporting the holdup of popular driver Nort Eddings, announced: "This stage robbing is getting very monotonous for the people of southern Oregon. If the robbers are caught this time a little 'hemp diet' would be a mild medicine."

Stage driver Nort Eddings *(left)* preparing to take a coach over the Siskiyous. *(Southern Oregon Historical Society)*

The San Francisco *Chronicle* ended a report of an 1877 Siskiyou stage robbery by adding: "We trust that energetic steps which are being taken to secure the arrest of the brigands will succeed so that the criminals will either stretch hemp or receive their quietus from the bullets of their pursuers' rifles. Unless this is done there can be no guarantee that these affairs will not be repeated as often as the Knights of the Road think it is necessary to replenish their purses at the expense of the public."

Siskiyou robberies followed the pattern of mountain holdups elsewhere. A heavy stage, pulled up a grade at a slow walk by laboring horses, would be suddenly challenged by one or two armed and masked road agents. The robbers usually stepped out from behind a large tree or rock and announced their intentions. Sometimes they remained concealed, showing only their shotgun or rifle. Most holdups took less than a minute. The robber would call to the driver to halt the coach. He would then command the driver to throw down the express box and perhaps the mail sacks. The drivers usually complied, as they were at a disadvantage with both hands full of reins and their own firearms tucked away. When the box and mail had been dropped to the road, the robber would order the driver to "move 'em along."

This simulated southern Oregon stage holdup mirrored the real thing.
(Josephine County Historical Society)

Sometimes a brazen road agent also would rob the passengers of whatever money and valuables they were carrying. If the loot was substantial, the robber was said to have "made a profit." But if the pickings were slim from the express box or pocket, the road agent made only a "water haul."

A rare and colorful account by a stage passenger of a moonlight robbery near the Siskiyou summit was printed in the June 28, 1878, edition of the *Ashland Tidings.* The passenger was Mr. J.C. Tolman of Ashland, Oregon. The southbound coach had left the Siskiyou Toll House after dark, and the seven passengers were enjoying the warm evening as the coach slowly climbed upward under a full moon.

Riding on top of the stage with the driver was a traveling drummer from the East on his first trip through the Siskiyous. It was obvious to the other passengers that the driver, Nort Eddings, was determined to entertain the Easterner as only stage drivers could. He was pointing out place after place of interesting note: there some cattle drivers were attacked by Indians; here some packers were murdered; there a stage was robbed.

The Eastern fellow had grown quiet, and then asked if there had been any stage robberies of late. The stage was approaching the summit and the driver assured him they were near the place of a recent robbery, when a hoarse voice called out from the side of the road, "Halt!" Two masked individuals appeared holding shotguns.

Tolman told the *Ashland Tidings:*

> Being on the inside, I did not understand what was the trouble, but supposed it to be a collision with the wagon of some belated teamster, and when the stage stopped I started to get out, and had succeeded in

getting my head and one foot out when I discovered the cause of our trouble. I next found myself back on the seat, trying to detach my watch from my vest, but totally failed to do so. I thrust it in my clothes and trusted that the robbers would not find it. I next threw my money under the seat. On a second thought, I took back $20, lest it might be considered too thin to be traveling on the stage without money.

My valuables being disposed of I ventured to peep out and see how matters stood. I found everything passing very quietly; driver very accommodating; two veritable robbers of more formidable aspect than any of my childish imagination had pictured. Two double-barreled shotguns pointed recklessly at the trembling passengers on the outside, completed the picture.

From my position, I could observe everything going on. The driver, with lines in one hand, was silently throwing out the mail bags—the express box had already been thrown down.

When the driver stopped throwing the bags out, the horses started, and the voice of a robber rang out on the dismal scene. "Is that all?" One of the robbers, to make sure, set his gun down and mounted the wheel to examine for himself. Right here I made up my mind never to travel on the stage again without a revolver. Had I one then, I could have killed both of the robbers. The one on the wheel I could have touched with a walking stick.

Soon the welcome orders came from the robbers for us to drive on. We were soon wheeling down the mountain at a good gait, with not a sound to be heard, save the beat of the horses' hoofs and the rattle of the coach over the gravel and corduroy road.

The most famous stage robber to operate in the Siskiyous was Mr. Charles E. Boles—Black Bart. Between

Dapper Charles Boles—alias Black Bart—robbed several gold-laden stagecoaches in Oregon's Siskiyou Mountains. *(Siskiyou County Museum)*

1875 and 1883 at least 28 stage drivers did business with him, and five of those meetings occurred on the Siskiyou grades. All of the drivers halted their lathered horses as they were bid and heard the five words with which Black Bart invariably announced his reason for stopping the stage: "Please throw down the box."

The courteous and dapper bandit-poet's story has been well-chronicled. Standing only five feet, seven and a half inches, this well-dressed little nemesis of Wells Fargo appeared less the road agent and more the successful businessman which, in a manner of speaking, he was.

But Boles was no friend to stage drivers. He was certainly no friend to Nort Eddings, who told the Jacksonville *Democratic Times* that he was "getting tired of the sport" after delivering the express box to Black Bart high in the Siskiyous on September 23, 1880. It was the third time robbers had called on Nort.

On the evening of November 20, 1880, near Cole's Station at the southern foot of the Siskiyous, driver Joe Mason was stopped by a highwayman holding a shotgun. He ordered Joe to hand out the mail and express box. Reporting the incident, the *Yreka Journal* noted: "The driver threw out the mail sack, but told the robber he would have to take the box out himself as it was hard to pull out from under the seat. The robber got up on the wheel and commenced trying to pull out the box. As he was doing so, Joe seized a hatchet and held it over the robber scaring him so badly that he desisted from any further efforts to get the box. Possibly he thought Joe's hatchet was a pistol, as he allowed him to start off without any further hinderance...He was evidently a *green hand, probably a tramp.*"

Green hand, indeed! Although he admittedly was having a bad day, it was later proved that the "green hand" was the notorious and experienced stage robber Black Bart.

Black Bart continued preying on Wells Fargo's treasure boxes until he was caught in 1883.

A few members of the Siskiyou Mountains "flour sack brigade" (as the *Yreka Journal* called them) who were brought to the bar of justice were Milt Shepardson, Bob Oliver, George Bouldin, Ben Berry, and the Wells brothers. Tom Brown, who robbed the southbound coach near Mt. Shasta, was tracked over the mountains to Ashland by Siskiyou County Deputy Sheriff John Hendricks and a Wells Fargo shotgun messenger, John Reynolds. Brown was arrested at a blacksmith's shop where he had stopped to get his horse shod. According to the *Ashland Tidings,* he told the lawmen if they had not been covering him with a shotgun he would have "riddled them with bullets."

As in most human endeavors, occasionally a holdup went amiss and the road agent was left with nothing for his efforts. On August 31, 1876, near the Oregon line, stage driver Milo Matthews came upon an obstruction of rocks and brush in the road. A passenger got out and cleared the way. "About that time," reported the *Yreka Journal,* "a voice in the bushes along the road called out to driver Matthews to throw out the express box. Milo politely informed the fellow to 'go to h--l,' and left at a lively gait. Nothing more was seen or heard of the would-be stage robber." The passenger's fate was not noted in the newspaper.

This Siskiyou Mountains ravine was a favorite with stage robbers.
(Authors' photo)

On June 16, 1882, a road agent invited Ellis Beggs to stop his northbound coach on the southern slope of the Siskiyous. The horses took fright at his sudden appearance and went downhill at a rattling pace, leaving the robber in the dust. He sent a bullet after the driver but missed.

Some of the road agents never made it out of the Siskiyous alive after robbing a stage. On November 24, 1876, John McNemar, a Wells Fargo messenger from Ashland and Yreka, found himself looking at a double-barreled shotgun on the Oregon side. The driver stopped the horses and John "Mac" handed down the treasure box. The bandit ordered the driver to go on. McNemar, not quite satisfied with the result, jumped down from the stage after it rounded a curve and went back to the scene of the robbery.

The Wells Fargo man saw the robber carrying the box into the trees. Slipping up to within fifty feet, he watched the road agent begin to open the box with a pick. McNemar let loose with one barrel of his shotgun, bringing the robber down with a hip wound. The highwayman grabbed for his own shotgun and McNemar let him have the other barrel, permanently removing Thomas Hunt from Wells Fargo's list of bandits.

Wells Fargo treasure box after a "roadside withdrawal." *(Siskiyou County Museum)*

The *Ashland Tidings* editor was of the opinion that McNemar's work was fair warning to other road agents, and announced: McNemar "deserves the gratitude of every community in the land for the wholesale terror his act will communicate to the gang of outlaws which are infesting our region."

Another shotgun messenger who forever ended a road agent's career was Wells Fargo's John Reynolds of Yreka. Soon after the Tom Brown capture, Reynolds was guarding the green box beside driver Charlie Williams at three o'clock on the morning of September 7, 1878. Their southbound coach had left Barron's Station on the Oregon side and the horses were laboring slowly toward the summit. It was dark in the mountains, and as the coach continued at a snail's pace up the grade Reynolds got down from the box and took a seat inside the coach. There had been a series of early morning holdups and the Wells Fargo man wanted to be ready.

Within a short distance of the summit a road agent called out that he had the driver covered and to halt the stage. Reynolds sat quietly in the coach as Charlie Williams stopped his team.

The robber moved closer to the stage and was illuminated by the coach lamp. Williams asked the highwayman to please lower his gun as he was unarmed and did not intend to resist. The request was granted. Just as the pistol was lowered, John Reynolds fired his shotgun from inside the coach, killing the robber instantly. The treasure box was saved and another road agent was retired.

The roadside withdrawal business was phased out when the railroad replaced stagecoaches in the Siskiyou Mountains in December 1887, but until then it remained a lively trade. Today's traffic on Interstate Highway 5 passes safely through the same forested and rocky canyons that once echoed the frightening command, "Throw down the box!"

Doc Le Burr and the Blue Mountains Stage Robbery

By the late 1860s, the eastern Oregon and southwest Idaho mining camps were pouring a continuous stream of golden treasure into the Oregon trade centers and on to San Francisco. Miners at the rich placer diggings of Boise Basin, Mormon Basin, Rye Valley, Clark's Creek, Auburn, and Sparta shipped the greater portion of their gold dust, nuggets, and bars on daily stages. Robberies by desperate and dangerous men were commonplace, but only one stage holdup is known to have been perpetrated by a physician.

In the summer of 1868, John Hailey's Pioneer Stage Line was running three stages daily between Umatilla and Boise City. The route of these treasure coaches passed over the Blue Mountains, southeast of Pendleton, with long grades perfect for use by the flour sack brigade.

One of Hailey's stage drivers, Seth Austin, had learned that some men whom he knew were planning a holdup. He reported his knowledge to Wells Fargo Agent Charles Woodward at Umatilla, who communicated the information to the Wells Fargo man at Uniontown (now Union), and John Hailey. A conference was also held with Umatilla County Sheriff Oscar F. Thomson and Postal Agent Brooks. It was decided that Austin, the stage driver, should try to find out the details of the robbery plan and report regularly to Woodward.

Through information from Austin, the officials learned the robbery would take place on August 2, somewhere on the east flank of the Blue Mountains. The lawmen set about preparing their surprise.

Late in the evening of August 1, the westbound stage was carrying the Wells Fargo treasure box as usual, but the contents were not so usual. On orders from Agent Woodward, over $7,000 in gold had been removed from the express box and replaced with rocks.

The stage left La Grande at two o'clock in the morning, carrying three passengers and driver Seth Austin, plus a Wells Fargo shotgun messenger named A.J. Sheppard. It also carried three bags of mail and the express box full of rocks.

The heavy coach stopped briefly to change horses at Pelican Stage Station, a few miles west of present Hilgard, and then began the slow climb toward Meacham. About daybreak, in a narrow canyon later known as Robber's Roost, four masked men suddenly appeared in the road and commanded the driver to stop. Two were armed with shotguns and two with rifles.

After finding only rocks in the treasure box, the foiled robbers ordered the driver to cut loose the two lead horses and go on without looking back. With only two horses to pull the coach, Seth Austin made slow progress up the steep grade. The stage finally reached Meacham Stage Station, where the robbery was reported.

A posse of lawmen who had been waiting there began tracking the outlaw band. The trail led the men eastward to the settlement of Summerville in the Grand Ronde Valley. They trailed the robbers to a farm owned by a leading Summerville citizen, Dr. William LeBurr, the town's popular physician. Here the robbers were arrested, some of them being already identified to the authorities by driver Austin. It was a shock and disappointment to the townspeople and the lawmen to learn that the estimable Doc LeBurr was the leader and chief organizer of the robber band.

Dr. LeBurr received a ten-year prison sentence, and upon his release from the penitentiary he did a strange thing. To the surprise of the community, he returned to Summerville and began to rebuild his medical practice. It did not go well for him at first, but when a devastating diphtheria epidemic swept the area, Doc LeBurr provided heroic and exhausting service to every patient needing his help. In the hearts of the townspeople he had atoned for his earlier veer off the path of morality and had reestablished himself as a valuable community resident.

Doc LeBurr was asked in later years why he returned to Summerville rather than seeking a fresh start elsewhere. He replied: "If you want to find something, the place to look for it is where you lost it."

Maxon and Berry: The Hidden Stage Treasure

In 1876, Mr. Lot Livermore was the Wells Fargo agent at Pendleton. Interviewed in his later years by Fred Lockley of the *Oregon Journal,* Mr. Livermore said: "In those days robbing stages was one of the recognized business enterprises of eastern Oregon." Two of the many roadside businessmen on the Umatilla-to-Boise City route were young Billy Maxon and Emory Berry.

On the 21st of October, 1876, Maxon and Berry robbed the westbound stage about six miles southeast of Umatilla. The mail sacks and passengers were not bothered, the boys contenting themselves with the $4,500 in gold from Wells Fargo's green box. The stage rolled on, and the bandit duo hightailed it out of there.

Following the stage road southeast toward Cayuse, Maxon and Berry approached the western slopes of the Blue Mountains, turned south, and traveled about twelve miles into the high country to the headwaters of McKay

Creek. There they made camp and hid out for several days.

Meanwhile, Wells Fargo Agent Lot Livermore and a party of lawmen followed the robbers' escape trail, a job made easier by a rainfall immediately before the stage holdup. But the trail was lost in the rough mountains.

Maxon and Berry decided to cache the gold near the camp, then work their way back down to the settlements to find out if they were in the clear. They hid the treasure, consisting of a gold bar, two buckskin bags of gold dust, and a baking powder can full of money, under a log.

Two nights later the robbers approached a farmhouse near Weston. Emory Berry stayed overnight at the farm, while Billy Maxon went into town to learn what was known about the stage robbery a week earlier.

Unfortunately for the young bandits, Lot Livermore and one of his possemen, John Bowman, were in town tracking down a rumor that two strangers had been seen heading out of the hills toward Weston. As Livermore and Bowman were putting up their buggy team in the livery stable, they noticed a horse that matched the description given by the stage driver. The liveryman said the owner of the horse, a stranger, was in Weston and he had heard that the man's partner had gone north over the line to Walla Walla. Bowman drove on toward Washington Territory to find him, while Lot Livermore hid in one of the livery stalls to wait for the owner of the horse.

Soon, however, Berry came riding into town from the farm where he had spent the night. He passed Maxon on the street without showing any sign of recognition, their prearranged signal that Billy should ride out to a meeting place and Emory would follow after a little while. Maxon went directly to the stable and ordered his horse. The liveryman gave a sign to the hidden Lot Livermore, and the

Wells Fargo man stepped out with his gun pointed at Billy. Lot later said that Maxon started to draw his gun, but realized it was futile. Livermore disarmed the stage robber, bound him, and put him in the custody of two local men he could trust.

Meanwhile, word reached Lot that Maxon's partner was having supper at the hotel. He went over to the hotel, got the drop on Berry, and marched him over to where Maxon was being held. Livermore returned to Pendleton, obtained a warrant for the arrest of the two, and sent the deputy sheriff to Weston to take them into custody.

Maxon and Berry denied knowing each other or anything about the stage robbery, but they were convicted and sentenced to ten years at hard labor in the Salem penitentiary. Shortly after the unlucky robbers began serving their time, they confessed their guilt and said they would reveal the hiding place of the stolen gold in exchange for lighter sentences.

They drew a map for Lot Livermore and gave him explicit directions: "Go to the elbow of the prairie just above our camp. You will find a dead pine—the only tree there. Look due east and you will see a large fir tree that has been stripped of its limbs on the south side by a falling tree. Near this big fir are two windfall trees. Under them you will find the treasure."

And there it was: two buckskin bags of gold, a gold bar, and a baking powder can full of currency. The boys won their lighter sentences and Lot Livermore was lauded by Wells Fargo.

The Burns and Goodrich Stage Robbery

In 1877 a similar stage robbery occurred in Umatilla County, but this time the golden harvest was never recovered. The holdup was near Cayuse Stage Station, on the Umatilla Indian Reservation. The villains in this roadside drama were two experienced bandits, Tom Burns and Alex Goodrich. The two road agents had a camp not far from the scene of the robbery, and it was later believed they had buried the loot—a gold bar and $3,000 in gold dust—somewhere near their camp.

Burns and Goodrich had made the mistake of hanging around the streets of Pendleton for several days prior to the holdup, and since they had no known occupation, they were noticed by law officers. After the robbery the two were arrested. They claimed to be horse buyers and denied any knowledge of the stage holdup, swearing they were not even in the area. But at their trial two Umatilla Indians testified that they visited the white men at a camp near the robbery site the morning after the stage was stopped. As they sat at the campfire with Burns and Goodrich, an ember from the fire blew onto Goodrich's hat, causing a burn in the material. The hat was produced by the prosecutor as evidence.

The two robbers were sentenced to the state penitentiary, and all attempts to get them to reveal the hiding place of the gold failed. Though both men continued to deny participation in the robbery, they did hint to officials that buried treasure could come in handy some day.

Alex Goodrich never again saw a free day for he died in prison of tuberculosis. Tom Burns was later released and he headed right back to Pendleton, where he soon disappeared and was never seen again. The popular theory was that Tom's pockets were probably quite heavy when he rode away.

As Oregon approached the twentieth century, the heyday of the stage robber faded. Holding up stages remained a lucrative business through the 1880s, but by 1890 most express treasure was sent by train, secured in locked and guarded cars. Some stage lines, however, still carried money and mail in areas not served by a railroad, and the road agents were still greedy.

In 1895 the Klamath Falls-to-Ager stage was robbed by a lone highwayman twelve times within a few months. The express company became so baffled at the numerous robberies that for a time it completely discontinued service on the line. Finally, on December 15, 1895, Bob Oliver was arrested as the road agent. There were several points of evidence linking him to the holdups, but two of the main factors that caused his downfall were his feet and those of his horse. It seems Oliver's right foot was crippled, leaving a track that pointed at almost a right angle to the imprint of the left foot. Such unique footprints were found at the robbery sites.

Oregon stage robber Bob Oliver *(right).*
(Siskiyou County Museum)

Also, Oliver's horse had only three shoes when Bob was arrested, and a three-shoe horse track was located near the last holdup scene. With that and other evidence, the jury retired Bob from his lucrative career. The Oregon Historical Society has Oliver's Marlin .38-caliber Model 1878 rifle, which he used in the holdups.

There were a number of latter-day stage robberies around Oregon, such as the holdups of the Oregon City-to-Salem stage, which was robbed three times in August 1895. In 1902, and again in 1903, the Roseburg-to-Myrtle Point stage was robbed, and in 1907 the Eugene-to-Florence coach was stopped by a shotgun-toting bandit. As late as 1913, the stage from Roseburg to Marshfield was held up near Coquille, with a grand total of $21 handed over to the robber.

Stage-robbing was a fool's errand in the later years, when the road agent received only a few dollars or nothing at all for his trouble. But at one time, making a roadside withdrawal from a gold-laden stagecoach in Oregon was the outlaw's way to easy riches—if he could stay ahead of the posse.

CHAPTER 3

Train Robbers Rode Free

Train robbing came into vogue with Western holdup artists in the late 1880s and lasted through the first few years of this century, when the iron horse steadily replaced stagecoaches as the preferred way to move money and bullion. Earlier, during the 1860s and 1870s, though there were a few train robberies, the average thief would be as likely to attempt holding up a volcano as a train. It was not an easy task to rob a train safely and get away with the goods. Trains carried many more people than did stages, and some of these passengers had guns and were not afraid to use them. Trains, unlike stagecoaches, usually had to be boarded while moving, then stopped and robbed.

The primary object of most train holdups was the express car, where the gold, valuables, and money was kept. Often the car was divided by a partition, the express section in front, mail to the rear. On some trains there was a separate mail car, and registered mail was a good bonus for the robbers, for it often contained money.

By the early 1890s, the usual place on a train for the robbers to board, as it puffed slowly up a grade, was on the

Robbers often used the "blind baggage" platform in front of the windowless express car to sneak aboard the train. *(Josephine County Historical Society)*

platform at the front of the windowless express car, just behind the tender. This small space became known as the "blind baggage," because someone hiding there could not be seen from the engine—the tender car full of coal or wood blocked the view—or from the express car. The platforms were intended to allow trainmen to walk down the entire length of the train while it was moving.

Once the robbers were on the blind baggage, they could climb over the tender and, with drawn guns, surprise the engineer and fireman in the cab. The train would then be halted, and the outlaws could attack the express car and, if they chose, enter the passenger cars to collect money and jewelry, usually with a trainman as hostage.

Robbing a train was a tough, dangerous undertaking, attempted by only the most brazen and desperate criminals. They were dramatic affairs, often punctuated by gunfire and in some cases death.

THE COW CREEK TRAIN ROBBERY

Late on the night of July 1, 1895, the Southern Pacific northbound train to Portland puffed its way through narrow, winding Cow Creek Canyon south of the town of Riddle in Douglas County. J.B. Waite was at the throttle and fireman Ev Gray stoked the big boiler. Suddenly, a loud explosion startled the trainmen. It seemed to come from under the front wheels of the engine. As Waite quickly set the air brakes, two more explosions were heard in the darkness—one ahead of the train, one to the rear. When the train stopped, a masked man appeared in the cab. Pointing a gun at Waite's head, he commanded the two to climb down to the ground and raise their hands.

Cow Creek Canyon was the Douglas County site of the Poole and Case train holdup on July 1, 1895.
(Authors' collection)

After scrambling down from the engine, the trainmen saw two more masked gunmen. The first robber marched the engineer and fireman back to the express car behind the tender. Fearing for the safety of Waite and Gray, Wells Fargo express messenger Donohue opened the express car door at the bandit's demand. Next came the mail car. The same masked man who visited the express car commanded the U.S. Mail messenger to open the door. He refused and the robber threatened to blow up the entire car with dynamite. The messenger then admitted the bandit and stood helplessly by with his hands raised as the outlaw ripped open the registered mail.

After obtaining money from the express and mail, the masked trio attacked the passenger cars. As the lead robber marched Waite and Gray through the cars of sleep-fogged, frightened passengers, the two others walked along the outside of the train, one on each side, periodically tossing lighted sticks of dynamite along the tracks to scare the people inside into cooperating.

The inside robber carried his gun in one hand and two cloth bags in the other. The passengers were ordered to deposit all their valuables into the bags. The Roseburg *Plaindealer* reported that he "kept up a lively conversation with the boys while they dumped their gold, silver, watches, and other valuables into two sacks provided for the occasion."

Though all the passengers were frightened, made more so by the outside explosions of dynamite every few minutes, a few were sufficiently cool and collected to secrete a portion of their money, keeping some out to quickly hand to the masked man as he passed in the aisle. One man, however, his thinking clouded by terror, slipped five dollars in silver into his shoe, but gave the robber ninety dollars in gold.

The inside thief showed at least a slight consideration toward certain passengers. The *Plaindealer* announced that "While it was a bold and dastardly affair, the robbers exhibited some redeeming traits. Women and children were unmolested and men who appeared to be workingmen were allowed to keep their money."

Then it was over. The gunman who had gone through the train herded the engineer and fireman back to the engine and ordered them not to proceed for two hours. Upon departing, one of the desperadoes shot out the train's headlight, and the robber band disappeared into the blackness of Cow Creek Canyon.

There was one small detail of which the bandit boss was unaware. He had worn a white cloth mask that hung down over his face with eye-holes cut in it. Several times during his march through the passenger cars, corners of the mask gently wafted away allowing six passengers and two trainmen to see his face. And they remembered it.

Early the next morning the hunt was on. Sheriff C.F. Cathcart, Riddle Constable George Quine, and a posse began searching the area of the holdup. Boot prints were found at the scene and leading away from it. They also came across horse tracks near the site and followed them to an abandoned camp in a willow thicket not far from the railroad tracks.

George Quine, a personable, bright country constable with a natural bent for detective work who would later be elected sheriff of Douglas County, noticed that one set of horse tracks showed a peculiar shoe design. Quine made a diagram of the horseshoe print, and also made note of the imprint designs of two sets of boots at the camp that matched those found at the holdup site.

Later that day, an area resident told officers he had seen James Poole and John Case heading in the direction of

Douglas County Sheriff George Quine was a constable in 1895 when he caught train robbers Jim Poole and John Case.
(Oregon State Sheriffs' Association)

the robbery location early on July 1, the day the train was held up. The lawmen gathered several additional pieces of evidence from the campsite, including cloth sacking material, string, and a number of gray horsehairs. Then they went looking for Poole and Case.

Jim Poole and John Case were well known to the law. Each had been guests of the state pen at Salem more than once, Poole for manslaughter and larceny and Case for assault with a deadly weapon and attempted robbery. In addition, both had been arrested frequently for minor crimes. They had met in prison in 1890, and when released—Poole in '92 and Case in '93—they lived on and off with Jim's father, Napoleon Poole, a respected Canyonville pioneer.

The two suspected train robbers were arrested on July

4. Jim Poole was taken at his father's house. His boots matched exactly the imprints found at the holdup scene and camp. Also, articles found in the Poole house, sacking and string, matched the items found in the camp. Case was arrested that same day in Canyonville. He had stabled Jim's gray mare in town, and Quine noticed that the horsehairs found at the Cow Creek camp matched those on the mare. And to clinch the matter, John Case's boots also fit the imprint design of a set of tracks at the robbery site.

Several of the holdup victims later identified John Case as the masked man who strode down the aisles of the cars, gun in hand, collecting their money and other valuables. Case and Poole were taken to Portland and held for trial in United States District Court on a charge of robbing the U.S. Mail. On Christmas Eve, 1895, the jury rendered a verdict of guilty. None of the stolen loot was ever recovered, and the third robber was never identified.

Train robber John Case.
(Authors' collection)

Old Bill Miner's First Train Robbery

In the award-winning 1983 motion picture he was called "The Grey Fox," and the title role was performed by the esteemed actor Richard Farnsworth. The movie presented a fairly accurate portrait of Old Bill Miner, the gentleman bandit who abhorred killing. And though the film took some historical liberties, it did depict a significant fact: Bill Miner pulled his first train robbery in Oregon.

Bill's entire adult life had been spent in crime or prison, beginning at the age of nineteen, when he held up

This is an 1888 San Quentin photo of Bill Miner, who robbed his first train near Portland in 1903. *(California State Archives)*

a store clerk and stole a horse in California. He quickly graduated to stage-robbing and over the years did business with a multitude of coaches in New Mexico, Colorado, and California. Bill was sent to San Quentin for three long stretches totaling thirty-three years.

During his last visit to San Quentin, from 1881 to 1901, Bill Miner took a fancy to a new specialty. Stages were on the way out; the big money now was carried on the twin ribbons of steel that crossed the country. Bill decided to learn the art of train-robbing. Fortunately, teachers of the craft abounded in San Quentin, and Bill was a patient listener.

It was during this time, too, that Miner met a fellow inmate who would later become his associate in Oregon: Jeplan Guy Harshman, a failed counterfeiter from San Francisco, who was lodged as a guest of the state for five years.

Miner left San Quentin for the last time on June 17, 1901. Where he spent the next couple of years is unknown, but on September 23, 1903, at an age when most men were contemplating a peaceful retirement, Old Bill Miner, nearly sixty, embarked on his new career.

Through the summer of 1903, Bill worked at the Four Brothers lumber mill near the Columbia River community of Goble, north of Portland. There he ran into his former fellow San Quentin inmate Guy Harshman. The idea of robbing a train had been percolating in both men for some time, and Harshman would later say that they talked about it daily for two weeks as they went about their mill work. A third man was needed and Bill recruited a young fellow whom he trusted, a petty thief named Charles "Kid" Hoehn.

Detailed plans were made to rob the express car of the eastbound Portlan-to-Chicago train. Kid Hoehn was sent to

Portland to steal a small boat, row it up the Columbia about eighteen miles, and hide it at a point near Troutdale. He then returned to Goble by train.

On Wednesday, September 23, 1903, the boys were ready. All three arrived in Troutdale, where their plan called for Miner and Harshman to wait for the evening train to come through. Meanwhile, Hoehn was to take the boat upriver about three miles from Troutdale and stash it just east of the railroad community of Corbett. He was then to stay hidden in the trees and brush, until the train arrived. It would be dark and he was to hold a lantern at trackside as a signal to the others, who would already be aboard. The robbery site, scouted in advance by Miner and Harshman, was on a curve at milepost twenty-one, just west of the Corbett tunnel.

The eastbound Oregon Railway & Navigation Co. No. 6 left Portland's Union Station at 8:15 p.m., right on schedule, with engineer Ollie L. Barrett and fireman H.F.

This curve, east of Corbett, was the site of the 1903 train-robbery by Bill Miner's gang. *(Authors' photo)*

Portland-Chicago No. 6, the train that started Bill Miner's train-robbery career. *(Oregon Historical Society)*

Stevenson. It puffed into Troutdale at a few minutes before nine o'clock that night, and when it pulled out, Bill Miner and Guy Harshman were hiding on the dark platform at the front of the express car.

Engineer Ollie Barrett would later relate the following events this way:

> About a mile beyond Troutdale two masked men climbed from the "blind baggage" over the tender and through the gangway into the engine, covering both Stevenson and myself with their revolvers. They ordered us to run the train to twenty-one mile post and stop at a light which would be found there. The bandits told us that if we kept still and obeyed orders, neither of us would be harmed, and we did so.
>
> At twenty-one mile post another masked man came out of the brush on the right hand side of the railroad and joined us as the train stopped.

Engineer Oliver Barrett was wounded in the attempted robbery of No. 6.
(Oregon Journal *photo)*

The engineer and fireman were ordered off the engine. They were instructed to hold two long willow poles, the ends of which had been tied to sticks of dynamite by Kid Hoehn while waiting for the train. Meanwhile, Miner and Harshman fired several shots to keep passengers inside. Conductor William Maher immediately went through the passenger cars, warning people to keep cool, stay seated, and to hide their money and valuables. Outside, the engineer and fireman were ordered to the express car, which on this train was a double compartment car: express in front, baggage to the rear, with doors to accommodate both functions.

Pacific Express messenger Fred A. Korner and his helper, Solomon Glick, had been busy attending to paperwork when the train slowed and stopped. Korner later said he thought something must have been wrong, so he turned out the lights, armed himself with a sawed-off Winchester shotgun, and waited.

Ollie Barrett was instructed by the robbers to tell the

express messenger to open the door. He called out: "It's Barrett. Open the door. Don't shoot." The demand had no effect, so the bandits took the dynamite poles from the trainmen, placed one against the door after lighting the fuse, and ushered their captives back to the engine.

The explosion blew a large hole in the front side-door, but did not injure the men inside, who had taken positions away from the door. As soon as the sound of the explosion died down, Barrett and Stevenson were ordered back to the express car by Miner and Harshman, while Kid Hoehn was off to the side watching the passenger cars.

As the party walked toward the express car, Fred Korner quietly opened the baggage door at the rear of the car. He aimed at the lead robber, who was about twenty feet away, and fired. One of the heavy pellets from Korner's

Express messenger Fred Korner on No. 6, who was considered a hero for protecting the train.
(Oregon Journal *photo)*

shotgun went through Harshman's chest and hit Ollie Barrett in the shoulder. Another ball struck Harshman in the head.

Harshman fell to the ground and Barrett yelled at Korner not to shoot anymore. None of the robbers returned fire. Seeing the job as a lost cause, Bill Miner ran with Kid Hoehn down the embankment toward the river. Korner came out of the express car, saw the robbers scrambling down the riverbank, and fired another blast from his shotgun but missed.

Ollie Barrett was helped onto the train, and it was backed up to Corbett, where dispatches announcing the robbery of No. 6 were immediately sent to Portland. James P. Nevins, Portland superintendent for the Pinkerton National Detective Agency, took charge of the case for the railroad, and Multnomah County Sheriff W.A. Storey led

James Nevins, Pinkerton's Portland superintendent. *(Pinkerton Archives)*

Sheriff W.A. Storey of Multnomah County led lawmen on the hunt for Bill Miner. *(Oregon State Sheriffs' Association)*

the police contingent. The combined posse of Nevins and his detectives and Storey and his deputies reached Corbett three hours later.

Guy Harshman was found along the tracks at the robbery site, badly wounded but alive, and was taken to Portland for treatment. The lawmen stayed at the scene until daybreak, searching as best they could by lantern light for traces of the escaped outlaws.

After daylight it was theorized that the robbers had fled by boat, for a bluff hundreds of feet high ran along the other side of the tracks, offering little chance of escape. The Columbia River, flowing at that time close to the tracks, provided the obvious way out. But to be thorough in their search, the posse combed the timber and farm country on top of the bluff, and for several miles each way along the railroad tracks.

On the Washington side of the Columbia, Clark County Sheriff Bert Biesecker and his men searched along the north side of the river for signs of the fugitives, though no trace was found.

Meanwhile, Harshman was not talking beyond giving his name as "Jim Conners." Under heavy guard at the hospital, he was constantly subjected to questioning by law officers for a number of days, but he refused to say anything about the robbery or the identity of his partners.

The Portland *Oregonian* reported on September 25, that: "The greatest interest Conners showed during the day was manifest at the time when his beard was shaved off and his hair trimmed, in order that the wound might be dressed. While the physicians were at work on him he swore enthusiastically, but stolidly refused to answer questions. His only desire to speak was to give voice to his feelings."

As the search continued, the O.R.& N. railroad posted a $500 reward for the arrest of each of the remaining bandits. That amount was increased when the Pacific Express Company also put up a $300 reward and the State of Oregon added another $300. (A state law enacted in 1878 provided for a reward of $300 for the arrest and conviction of any person obstructing or illegally stopping a railroad train in the state.)

After an intensive investigation of Jim Conners by Pinkerton detectives, it was determined that his real name was Jeplan Guy Harshman, a counterfeiter and ex-convict from California. It was also learned that upon his release from San Quentin in 1892, Harshman was arrested in Seattle, again for making bad money, and sentenced to a

Jeplan Guy Harshman, one of Bill Miner's gang, was shot during the September 23, 1903 train robbery.
(Oregon Journal *photo)*

term at McNeil Federal Penitentiary in Washington. Faced with these facts, and desirous of cooperating with the authorities in hopes of a lighter sentence, Harshman gave up the names of his two confederates.

About a week after the robbery, Kid Hoehn was arrested in an Everett, Washington hotel room. From him the lawmen learned what had happened after the holdup. Upon scrambling down the embankment, Miner and Hoehn had quickly rowed across the river, then drifted and rowed downriver to Kalama on the Washington side. There they left the boat and took to the woods, where they remained in hiding for several days. Then they separated, going by different routes to the Puget Sound country. Hoehn swore he had never again seen Bill Miner after they parted. That was probably true, since Bill kept going all the way to Canada and to further adventures with trains.

Guy Harshman was sentenced to twelve years in prison for the holdup of Portland-Chicago No. 6, and Charlie "Kid" Hoehn was sentenced to a term of ten years.

Almost exactly one year later, on September 10, 1904, Old Bill Miner and two new companions pulled the first train robbery in the history of Canada. The British Columbia holdup netted Bill and his friends $7,000. Next, Bill robbed a Great Northern train near Seattle, and in the spring of 1906 he held up a Canadian Pacific train near Kamloops, British Columbia.

The old highwayman was arrested for the Canadian Pacific job and sentenced to life in prison. He broke out a year later and continued doing business with railroad and express companies in Canada and the United States until he was caught in February 1911 after a train holdup in Georgia. But the slippery old-timer escaped later that year and was not recaptured for over a year.

When he was again in irons, the man whom the Pinkertons called "The Gentleman Bandit" told Pinkerton official Henry Minster, "You know, I'm getting too old for this sort of work."

Old Bill Miner died in a prison hospital on September 1, 1913 at the age of sixty-seven.

Bad Day at Kamela

In the first years of this century, it was the strict policy of railroads to safety-test their engines' air brakes on the summit of mountain ranges before rolling down the steep grades. For the test, a trainman went to the rear of the last car, while the engineer let the train attain the speed of a running man and applied the air, bringing the train to a stop. The checker, standing on the rear platform, would determine that the brakes worked properly on the last car, thus showing that they worked all through the train. He would then signal the engineer to go ahead.

Such a test was always made at Kamela Station on the

summit of the massive Blue Mountains of eastern Oregon. If the air brakes checked out all right, a westbound train would proceed down to Pendleton, and an eastward running train would roll down toward La Grande.

The railroad policy of testing air brakes was the reason on July 2, 1914, at a few minutes before one o'clock in the morning, three men were concealed in bushes along the tracks at Kamela.

Charlie Manning, Al Meadors, and Clarence Stoner were train robbers. At least they wanted to rob one particular train, the westbound Oregon-Washington Railway & Navigation Company's "Fast Mail" No. 5. The No. 5 was known to usually contain much treasure in the express and mail cars, and it was an appetite-whetting delight to those bent on banditry.

Manning, the big, startlingly handsome, dark-haired leader of the band of desperadoes, was an accomplished robber from Cokeville, Wyoming, who ran with the outlaw Whitney brothers in Idaho and Wyoming. Clarence Stoner and Al Meadors had no known criminal records, though Clarence was the son of Abe "Rocky" Stoner, an associate of Butch Cassidy and the Wild Bunch.

What Charlie, Al, and Clarence did not know, however, was that the railroad had just issued new timetables with a printing error, and trains 5 and 23 were reversed on the schedules. The train now approaching Kamela, showing on the schedule as No. 5, was actually No. 23, a passenger train running leisurely from Salt Lake City to Portland. The Fast Mail would be along later. The robbers were waiting for the wrong train.

As the train appeared and slowed to a stop, the boys got ready. The brake test was performed, and rear brakeman Frank Earle signaled the engineer that all was okay and he could go ahead. Just as the train began

The site of the Manning Gang robbery in the Blue Mountains. *(Authors' photo)*

chugging away from Kamela Station, the masked bandits quickly ran out of the bushes and boarded the front end of the last car.

The train continued on as the robbers marched brakeman Earle ahead of them at gunpoint, collecting conductor William Fergus, brakeman Clyde Enock, and three Pullman porters on the way to the front. Though the express car usually was locked all around, American Express messenger C.W. Cramp had just unlocked the rear door because he was expecting the brakeman to come forward and help him unload express packages at the Meacham depot a few miles ahead.

Stoner held the trainmen at gunpoint in the express car while Manning and Meadors went up to the engine and ordered engineer Fred Johnson to stop the train. He and the fireman were then brought back to the express car.

Charlie Manning told the express messenger he wanted all that was in the two safes. Cramp provided a key

Train robbers: Clarence Stoner *(left)* and Al Meadors *(right)*.
(Oregon State Archives)

to the smaller safe and Manning extracted $200 in gold and currency. But the large safe had no combination dial and Cramp explained that it had been taken off and was not in the car. Manning then opened a bag to show a dozen sticks of dynamite, saying that he would blow the safe open. But Cramp convinced the angry outlaw that there was nothing of value in the safe.

Manning then instructed Stoner to keep the train crew guarded in the express car while he and Meadors returned to rob the passengers. Meadors led the way, holding a large cloth bag for the collection. Manning followed with a gun in each hand.

There were eleven passenger cars on the train, including day coaches, dining car, chair car, sleepers, and a smoking car. The bandits worked their way through the first cars, demanding and receiving money, watches, and jewelry from the frightened passengers. No one resisted and the robbery was going smoothly for the boys, until they reached the end of the third car.

Morrow County Deputy Sheriff George McDuffee was on his way back to Heppner from Canyon City, where he had been a witness in a horse stealing case. He was sitting in the last tier of seats on the left side of the train. As the robbers walked past him, McDuffee pretended he was asleep, and for some reason they did not wake him for his contribution.

Just as Meadors and Manning opened the vestibule door leading from McDuffee's coach to the next car, the plucky deputy stood, pointed his gun at Manning, and shot twice. Both bullets hit the big bandit, but he fired three times at McDuffee. One of the shots hit the lawman in the right chest, but was miraculously deflected by a brass pencil case and a deck of cards in his breast pocket. The

Charlie Manning, killed during the Kamela train robbery.
(Authors' collection)

pencil case caused the bullet to range downward and come out just above his hip instead of going through his heart.

McDuffee was stunned by the wound, but managed to get off two more shots at the outlaw. He later told the *Oregon Journal:* "My cartridges were loaded with black powder and made a big smoke. I am satisfied that they could not see me very well because of the smoke." One of McDuffee's last shots struck Charlie Manning in the head. He fell into the vestibule and died.

Meanwhile, Al Meadors, who had preceded Manning into the vestibule, did not fire a shot. He had given his gun to Manning for the walk through the coaches. By the time he grabbed one of the guns from his dead leader, he figured it was time to get off the train.

Meadors jumped to the ground and ran up to the express car, yelling for Clarence Stoner to get out of there. Stoner joined him on the ground, and the two men ran into the forest. They camped in the woods five miles from the holdup scene and hid there all the next day. They cached most of the stolen loot nearby, keeping some of the money with them, and the following night they began walking out to La Grande.

The robbery had occurred in the northeast corner of Umatilla County, the bailiwick of Sheriff Til Taylor, and the Blue Mountains were soon being combed by a large posse of lawmen and volunteers. There was no clear trail to follow, but with the tracks and roads closely watched, it was believed that the two remaining train robbers would not escape.

On July 4, about 9:30 in the morning, Union County Deputy Sheriff Batcheler was watching the railroad tracks seventeen miles east of the holdup site. Two men came into view walking along the tracks, and because they matched the general description of the fugitives, Deputy Batcheler detained them at gunpoint. They had $355 on them, and when a few questions were asked, the men's evasive answers prompted the deputy to take them into La Grande for further investigation.

During questioning by Sheriff Taylor and railroad Chief Special Agent E.B. Wood, the two suspects broke down. They gave their names as Al Meadors and Clarence Stoner and admitted they had robbed the train at Kamela with Charlie Manning. While the nation celebrated Independence Day, Meadors and Stoner sat morosely in irons, their own freedom a thing of the past. They later led officers to the hidden loot and pled guilty in Umatilla Circuit Court. Each was sentenced to thirteen years in the Oregon State Penitentiary.

Murder at Tunnel 13

The most notorious and tragic train robbery ever to take place in the West occurred in Oregon on October 11, 1923. It shook the Northwest like an earthquake and its aftershocks were felt all over the nation and beyond.

At the top of the Siskiyou Mountains in southern Oregon there is a 3,108-foot tunnel that bores through the uppermost crest of that massive barrier range. It was constructed for the railroad in 1887 and was given the prophetic numerical designation "Tunnel 13." At the north portal of this tunnel, hard on the Siskiyou summit, all southbound trains paused to perform their air brake test before rolling down the southern slope of the mountains into California.

In the late morning of October 11, 1923, the Southern Pacific passenger and mail train en route from Seattle to San Francisco, dubbed the "Gold Special" for its Northwest mines bullion shipments, pulled into Ashland at the foot of

Southern Pacific No. 13, the "Gold Special," near Ashland.
(David Ramstead collection)

the Siskiyous. Ironically, the train's number designator was the same as the tunnel it would climb toward.

Ashland was the changing point for the train's crew; the fellows from the north were replaced by a fresh team from the Shasta Division. The engineer was fifty-one-year-old Sidney Bates, and his fireman was Marvin Seng, just twenty-three. The brakeman, Coyle Johnson, was to celebrate his thirty-eighth birthday on the following day. Conductor C.O. Merritt, mail clerk Elvyn Dougherty, and baggage clerk Jim Huffy rounded out the main crew.

At noon the Gold Special moved out of the station to begin slowly winding its way up to Tunnel 13. It was assisted up the mountain by a helper engine that would be uncoupled north of the tunnel before the brake test was done. During the upward pull, which took about half an hour, the passengers and crew relaxed and enjoyed the scenery on a pleasant, blue-sky day.

When No. 13 reached the top, the helper engine was taken off and Sid Bates ran his brake test. None of the crew noticed the two men hunched down in the trackside bushes near the north portal of the tunnel. Both men were armed and their faces were covered with black greasepaint. On the south side of the tunnel another man crouched in hiding, his face also blackened. He was armed with a shotgun. Nearby was a cache of dynamite.

Satisfied with the air brake test, Bates slowly eased the throttle forward in the cab of No. 13 and proceeded toward the nearby tunnel. As he did so, the two men sprang from their place of concealment and jumped aboard the platform on the mail car. Then they climbed over the tender and into the engineer's cab.

Bates and Seng were startled by the sudden appearance of two armed men, one holding a .45 and the

Tunnel 13, site of the infamous DeAutremont train robbery and murders on October 11, 1923. *(David Ramstead collection)*

other a shotgun. Engineer Bates was ordered to continue on into the tunnel and stop exactly when the engine's cab emerged from the south portal. He did so. No. 13 hissed noisily to a stop as the engine came out of the south end of Tunnel 13.

The two young men in the cab were brothers Roy and Hugh DeAutremont; Roy was twenty-three, Hugh nineteen. The fellow on the ground at the south end of the tunnel was Ray DeAutremont, Roy's twin brother. The DeAutremont brothers, petty thieves and n'er-do-wells, thought of themselves as a latter-day Jesse James gang, and they wanted to pull the West's last great train robbery. Also, the brothers wanted to be wealthy, a goal they reckoned could be realized through Uncle Sam's Postal Service car on the Gold Special.

Roy and Hugh ordered the engineer and fireman to the ground, while Ray took the dynamite back to the mail car. As the young robber approached, mail clerk Elvyn Dougherty stuck his head out to see what was going on. Ray blasted at him with his shotgun. Dougherty ducked back inside and locked the door.

Jim Huffy, in the baggage car attached behind the mail car, also looked out. Both mail and baggage cars were still in the tunnel and Huffy cautiously slid the door open just enough to look ahead to the engine. When he saw Marvin Seng with his hands in the air and heard the shotgun, Huffy knew a robbery was taking place. He quietly closed the door and kept still.

Roy DeAutremont left Hugh to guard the engineer and fireman and ran back to help Ray with the dynamite. The nervous, sweating young bandits demanded that the mail clerk open the door. Dougherty refused. They then placed the explosives against the mail car door, figuring the tunnel would muffle the sound of the blast. Using a

DuPont plunger-type detonator, they touched off the dynamite.

The train had been stopped for several minutes and conductor C.O. Merritt and brakeman Coyle Johnson had gone forward to see what was the matter. Suddenly, a deafening explosion shook the cars and blew out all the train's windows. The tunnel rapidly filled with smoke. The passengers, seated in the dark cars further back in the tunnel, were numbed with fear and confusion, and some were injured by flying glass.

Merritt and Johnson, joined by a few others,

The DeAutremonts set a dynamite charge that blew apart the mail car, killing the postal clerk. *(David Ramstead collection)*

continued working their way toward the front of the train, their path illuminated by a fusee railroad flare. Soon, however, all but Coyle Johnson turned back. The robbers had used too much dynamite and the mail car was ripped to shreds and on fire. Jim Huffy, in the next car back, lay unconscious but alive. Mail clerk Elvyn Dougherty was not so lucky. He died in the explosion, and his body was incinerated in the resulting fire.

As Coyle Johnson came running toward the end of the tunnel, he ran smack into the pointed gun of a mad Roy DeAutremont. He ordered Johnson to uncouple the mail car from the rest of the train, but because of the blast damage the brakeman could not get the car unhooked. Roy then ordered him to run up to the engine and tell the others to have the engineer pull the train a short way out of the tunnel.

As the frightened man ran up to the engine with his hands raised, though, Ray DeAutremont leveled his shotgun and blasted Johnson in the midsection. Johnson fell and Ray went up to him and shot him again.

Roy then came out of the tunnel and after a quick consultation the brothers ordered engineer Bates back up to the engine with instructions to move the train ahead. Hugh accompanied the engineer, keeping a .45 aimed at his head. Bates tried to move the train forward, but it would not budge. With the mail car still in the tunnel, the frustrated robbers could not get into it, and it looked like everything inside was burned.

Now enraged beyond control, the three desperadoes were even more ruthless. Roy shot the fireman, Marvin Seng, twice at close range with a .45. As the terror-stricken Sid Bates sat in the cab, Hugh killed him with a shot to the head. The crazed robbers-turned-killers had murdered four men, injured others, and had received not one cent in the

$15,900 Reward *in Gold*

ROY A. A. DE AUTREMONT
Picture taken early in 1923

RAY CHARLES DE AUTREMONT
Picture taken in 1920
He now resembles closely his twin brother Roy

HUGH DE AUTREMONT
Picture taken in 1923

ROY A. A. DE AUTREMONT, alias R. A. Harris, alias R. A. Burton, age 23 in 1923, weight 135-140 pounds, height 5 feet 6 inches. Complexion medium light. Hair medium light brown. Eyes peculiar looking, narrow and squinty, light brown. Wears glasses in reading. Face broad at the cheek bones. Nervous, and a "dreamer." Likes to argue against the Bible. Long, turned up nose and prominent nostrils. Tonsils have been removed. Head round. Wears No. 6 shoe. Boastful and egotistical. Clips his words. Forward and presuming with women. First upper right molar tooth has amalgam filling, as have both first right and left lower molars.

RAY DE AUTREMONT, alias R. C. Burton, alias William Elliott, alias Chas. R. Joseph, age 23 in 1923. Height 5 feet 6 inches. Weight 135-140 pounds. Complexion medium light. Hair medium light brown. Broad face. Prominent nostrils. Short cut neck. Eyes, peculiar looking, light brown, small and squinty. Wears glasses when reading. Big toe nail on left foot turned up. Cut scar at tip of left forefinger inner, and at back of second joint right middle finger, also round cut scar back of head. Gold foil in upper left cuspid, mesial surface. Amalgam filling, upper left first molar, occlusal surface. Gold inlay, upper right cuspid, mesial and incisive angle.

HUGH DE AUTREMONT, alias E. E. James, alias Hugh DeKay, alias Hugh De Lerious, alias Hugh DeCoy. Age 19 in 1923, looks older. Height 5 feet 7 inches. Weight about 135 pounds. Complexion fair, eyes blue. Nose slightly pug. Hair medium light, slightly sandy and curly. Amalgam filling right and left molars, and same in first right upper molar. Likes to argue and is good debater. Fond of sports, particularly boxing and running. Expressed desire for traveling, and has boasted of trips he has made by riding freight trains. He is bright and alert and has a high school education. Little fingers turn outward at first joint.

REWARDS totaling $15,900 (*$5,300 FOR EACH MAN*) are offered for information leading to the arrest and conviction of these men, who are wanted for the holdup of train near Siskiyou, Oregon, and the murder of the railway postal clerk and three trainmen on October 11, 1923

▼

COMMUNICATE INFORMATION TO YOUR POSTMASTER, TO PEACE OFFICIALS, AND TO

C. RIDDIFORD,
Post Office Inspector in Charge
Spokane, Wash.

D. O'CONNELL,
Chief Special Agent, Southern Pacific
Company, San Francisco, Calif.

DeAutremont wanted poster. *(David Ramstead collection)* robbery. They fled from the area into the wild mountain country of the Siskiyous to hide.

Meanwhile, the explosion of the mail car was not muffled—it had been heard for several miles in every direction. Crews from railroad maintenance camps on both the Oregon and California sides of the Siskiyous were en route to Tunnel 13. It was not long before the word went out to the authorities of the carnage.

Jackson County Sheriff Charles Terrill, based in Jacksonville, took charge of the case. He quickly formed a huge posse, broke men into groups, and began scouring the mountains. On the California side, Siskiyou County Sheriff Calkins did likewise. The lawmen were to be assisted by Southern Pacific's famed Chief Special Agent Dan O'Connell, who, with a party of agents, hurried by special train to Oregon from his San Francisco office. On the next day, October 12, a detachment of thirty troops from the Oregon National Guard moved into the area to assist the lawmen. Soon hundreds of armed searchers were scattered through the Siskiyous.

A slip of paper with Roy's and Hugh's names on it had been left in a pair of coveralls discarded at the scene. The paper, a registered letter receipt, had a Eugene, Oregon postmark. A check in that town by detectives produced an elderly barber named Paul DeAutremont, who said he had three sons: Roy, Ray, and Hugh. Additional evidence found at the scene positively linked the three boys with the train massacre. Now the lawmen had names, descriptions, and photographs to help their manhunt.

But time passed without a trace of the killers. Lawmen were plagued with false leads and sightings, but the quarry remained at large. Months turned to years and the big murder case went from headlines to back-page items, then faded away. Finally, in 1926, a chance perusal of some Post

Hugh DeAutremont (straw hat) arrived in Medford handcuffed to Sheriff Ralph Jennings of Jackson County. *(David Ramstead collection)*

Office wanted posters by a soldier in San Francisco led to the arrest of Hugh DeAutremont in Manilla, Philippines, where he was serving as an army private under an assumed name.

Hugh's arrest renewed interest in the DeAutremont case and spurred new publicity. In a small Ohio town a man saw the newspaper accounts of the deadly brothers and recognized photos of Roy and Ray as men he worked with nearby. The two were arrested in Steubenville, Ohio, where they were living under the names Clarence and Elmer Goodwins.

The three brothers were eventually returned to

Captured train robbers Ray Deautremont *(right front)* and twin brother, Roy *(rear)*. *(David Ramstead collection)*

Oregon. Hugh's trial in Jacksonville resulted in a conviction for first-degree murder. Roy and Ray arrived in Jacksonville under close guard during their brother's trial, and when he was convicted, they broke down, admitted their guilt, and gave statements detailing the events on that afternoon at Tunnel 13.

Each of the DeAutremont brothers was sentenced to life in prison. Hugh was paroled in January 1959 and moved to San Francisco, where he died several months later. Ray was paroled in 1961 and worked as a janitor in Eugene, where he died in a rest home. Roy DeAutremont never did see another free day. He was declared incurably insane in 1949 and given a lobotomy. He was transferred to the Oregon State Hospital, where he remained until his death.

The 1923 Tunnel 13 holdup was the last train robbery in Oregon.

CHAPTER 4

HANK VAUGHAN: NATIVE SON-WITH-A-GUN

OCCASIONALLY IN THE OLD WEST a man was so known for his nerve and quick gun that his reputation became his identity. The legacies of these men—Hickok, Hardin, Bonney, the Earps, and others—are the legends that live from one generation to the next. They were gunfighters, men whose often mundane lives were accented by sporadic incidents of gunsmoke and death. They made good press in their day, and still find a wide audience in ours. In Oregon, such a man was Hank Vaughan—one of the Northwest's most colorful badmen.

Over a century after his death, we can provide only a sort of sketchbook of Hank's wild, unpredictable exploits. It cannot be a complete biography because much of his daily life was not recorded or has been lost. And, besides, Hank's days spent in peaceful pursuits, like those of most gunfighters, and the years he operated a large wheat farm in Umatilla County—these are not the reasons that stories are still told of Hank Vaughan. It was his propensity to slap leather, coupled with a knife-edge temper and a quirky sense of right and wrong, that whets our interest.

Legends about Vaughan abound today among eastern

Oregon old-timers, though none are left who knew him firsthand. The facts about some of his exploits are difficult to ascertain, though the stories that follow have been documented as closely as possible and are substantially true. If some of the tales have grown just a bit in the telling over the years, it's all right. Hank would have liked it that way.

Not much is known of Vaughan's early years, as he was not inclined to give his historical antecedents. It is known, however, that he was born Henry C. Vaughan on April 27, 1849, near Coburg in Oregon's Willamette Valley. (Some writers have spelled Hank's last name "Vaughn," after a common misspelling in contemporary newspapers. Hank always spelled it "Vaughan.")

Hank's first recorded gunplay occurred in 1864 at Canyon City. He was about fifteen years old. Daniel M. Taylor, commonly called Matt, later a lawman in eastern Oregon, was there and saw it. In an interview in 1926 with the *Oregon Journal's* Fred Lockley, Matt Taylor said that Vaughan had been drinking and was having a dispute with one William Headspot. Hank suddenly pulled his gun and shot Headspot in the head, killing him. Shootings were so common in the wide-open gold camp that no charges were brought against young Vaughan—at least there is no record of any legal action.

The next year he killed again, and this time the consequences were different. In the spring of 1865, Hank was camped at the Express Ranch on the Burnt River in Baker County with a companion, Dick Bunten. They had stolen a herd of horses and were en route to Idaho. Sheriff Frank Maddock of Umatilla County, where the horses were stolen, had been trailing the two rustlers and came upon their camp at night. Riding with Sheriff Maddock was his deputy, O.J. Hart.

When the lawmen approached the camp, Vaughan and Bunten were asleep. Instructing Hart to handle the boy (Hank), Maddock jerked the blankets off the sleeping forms. Hank and his partner came up shooting and the officers shot back. Bunten was killed instantly, as was Deputy Hart, who was shot by Vaughan.

The young outlaw then shot Sheriff Maddock. The wound was not fatal, however, as the bullet passed through Maddock's cheek and middle ear, emerging at the base of the skull. Maddock was able to shoot Hank, though not critically, before he fell. Vaughan then beat the fallen sheriff on the head with his gun and rode into the night.

The next morning a group of miners came to the grisly scene, where they found the two dead men and the severely wounded sheriff. Maddock was taken to a mining camp, and before long a posse of miners went looking for Vaughan. His escape had been slowed by his wound and he was soon captured.

Hank was taken to Auburn, the county seat of Baker County, where he was indicted on May 25 for murder and theft. Justice moved quickly in those days; on May 29 he was found guilty of murder in the second-degree and the next day he was sentenced to life in prison at hard labor.

On the evening of the 30th, a large crowd of Auburn miners, believing the young killer had gotten off too easy, came to the jail with a rope. Calmer heads prevailed, though, and the mob dispersed. Hank was transported to Portland, where the state penitentiary was then located (it was moved to Salem in 1866) and he entered the gate on June 14, 1865 as convict number 172.

Vaughan was a model prisoner, learned the blacksmith trade in the prison shop, and, despite his life sentence was released with a pardon on February 22, 1870. It is believed that upon his release he went to Nevada and Utah, where he worked as a blacksmith for a number of years.

There were rumors that he was involved in several temper-spawned, violent incidents while in Nevada, including the killing of two or three men. Also, an outlaw named William Roe claimed in a confession that he and Hank Vaughan held up a stage in Idaho in those early years. The Roe statement was made much later, in November 1896, when Roe was in custody for murder in California. But nothing in the robbing line was ever charged to Hank.

Later Vaughan abandoned the blacksmith trade to become a dealer in horses. With partners Still Huelet and Bill Moody, Hank sold horses at a profit in eastern Oregon, though where they obtained the stock was sometimes in doubt.

Hank Vaughan was one of the Northwest's most colorful badmen. *(Oregon State Sheriffs' Association)*

Like many men who were quick with a gun, Hank got into shooting scrapes because of his temper and his drinking. His physical appearance alone was not fearsome, for he was a small man weighing only about 130 pounds, including his shooting iron. His clothing ran to that of a clergyman or gambler: black broadcloth frock coat, vest, black trousers, white shirt, and black string tie. And he always went armed.

Hank loved jewelry. He habitually wore several rings and a conspicuous gold chain, which went around his neck, the ends fastened to a gold watch. According to his attorney William Parsons, who knew him well, Hank for some time kept a private safe in the Transfer Hotel in Pendleton. In the safe he stored many assorted and valuable rings, diamond pins, gold studs, gold nuggets, money and his collection of a dozen or more beautifully mounted revolvers.

Eastern Oregon, primarily the Pendleton-Athena area of Umatilla County, was Hank's home ground for many

The community of Athena, where Hank Vaughan rode his horse through the saloons. *(Umatilla County Historical Society)*

years. It was there, in the 1880s saloons and gambling dens of Athena, Weston, Adams, and Pendleton, that he gained much of his reputation for cussedness. His antisocial habits of riding horses into the saloons, shooting out lights, blasting beer glasses off bars, and generally shooting his gun whenever and wherever he felt like it, inside or out, made Hank Vaughan a less than welcome guest—a friend to the rowdy crowd, a terrorizing ruffian to others.

At other times, Hank was a peaceful, law-abiding citizen, generous and open. But even then it was prudent to keep on his good side. It's a sure bet that Charley Long wished he had.

The Charley Long-Hank Vaughan duel, in its various versions, was the apex of Hank's checkered career. Nothing in all the history of gunfighting is stranger.

Hank moved down to Prineville for awhile in 1881, just drifting along, gambling some and drinking plenty. One day in 1882, Hank was sitting in the Til Glaze Saloon drinking and playing cards with a local gunfighter and vigilante, Charley Long. There were angry words between them, then shouts and swearing. Some who later claimed to have been there, and others who knew Hank, believed the trouble arose over jealousy between Long and Vaughan over who was the struttingest rooster.

In any event, things soon got out of hand, and they agreed on a fight to the finish. Each took hold of one end of a large scarf or handkerchief, so the story goes. Then they pulled out their guns, and right there in the middle of the saloon began shooting at each other, every shot taking effect. Both men were wounded several times at that close distance, but they both recovered.

Another account was reported to *The Dalles Times* by an alleged eyewitness. In this version the two men

Hank Vaughan's Colt .44–40. *(Oregon State Sheriffs' Association)*

"grabbed left hands and emptied their revolvers at each other."

The duel was remembered a differently, however, by James M. Blakely, who was indeed there. He was later elected the first sheriff of Crook County and was respected for his honesty. According to a 1939 *Oregonian* interview, Blakely said the fight occurred on a Sunday morning after a local horse race. Blakely and Sam Smith were in the Dick Graham Saloon and saw Vaughan at a table with Long. Blakely knew both men; he was friendly with Hank, but did not care for Long. The two were just sitting there playing cards and drinking.

Blakely and Smith left to take care of some business, and when they returned to town that afternoon, they saw Hank and Charley in the Til Glaze Saloon, drinking and talking. Their conversation became heated, and pretty soon they went out to the middle of the floor and started shooting at each other. Blakely did not recall any grasping of hands or handkerchief. He said Hank was shot twice and Long was hit three times.

Which version is correct? Blakely, though known for honesty, related an incident that occurred fifty-seven years earlier. Other accounts were more contemporary with the event, and it surely was like Hank Vaughan to grab a corner of a scarf, pull his iron, and go to shooting. Particularly if he was well-oiled and mad.

It is undisputed that one of the shots struck Hank in the chest and that many thought he would die. When the first news of the shooting came to Vaughan's home country in Umatilla County, it was said to be probably fatal, and some of the people around Pendleton and Athena felt like celebrating.

The Pendleton *East Oregonian* ran an item to the effect that Hank had shaken hands with fate in his Prineville encounter and was about to be measured for a "shroud and a plank overcoat." But such was not the case. Hank recuperated in Prineville, then moved back to Umatilla County. Upon his arrival in Pendleton he chased the *East Oregonian* newspaper editor, J.P. Wagner, out of his office for printing such a story.

Charley Long also recovered and later went up to Washington, where he was killed by a rancher.

Vaughan was shot in the chest on one other occasion, this time right in his home town of Athena, then known as Centerville. Hank had certain unsociable quirks that sometimes made it difficult to like him. It was his custom upon seeing a stranger in a saloon, if Hank was full of something distilled, and he often was, to make the man "dance." If the stranger declined, Hank punctuated his request with several shots close to the man's feet. That usually got them kicking up smartly.

One day in 1886, while Hank was in the Blue Front Saloon, a stranger named W.H. Falwell came in. When Hank's command to dance went unheeded, he opened fire with his six-shooter around Falwell's feet. The latter then began stepping nimbly. Afterward, Hank stood drinks all around, considering the incident closed. Unfortunately for Vaughan, Falwell was not a man to be trifled with in such a cavalier and embarrassing manner. He left the saloon, procured a pistol, and returned to get Vaughan. Meanwhile, Hank had gone over to the Hollis & Cleve store, where Falwell found him.

Without any prefatory remarks, Falwell began shooting. One slug shattered Vaughan's right arm and another caught him in the chest, puncturing a lung. In shock, Hank made his way behind a stand of thread spools. The irate stranger continued shooting until his gun was empty, then left the store. Again, Hank recovered from his wounds. Falwell went to prison for two and a half years on a conviction of assault to kill.

A few weeks after the shooting, Hank's lawyer, Colonel William Parsons, visited him on some legal business. As Parsons entered the Vaughan ranch house, a stepdaughter cautioned him to be careful about going into Hank's room

Hank Vaughan was shot in this Athena store by W.H. Falwell.
(Umatilla County Historical Society)

as he was target practicing. Indeed, the lawyer found him propped up by pillows, a gun in his left hand and several boxes of cartridges on the bed. Hank told Parsons, interspersed with loud, smoky blasts from his hand-cannon, that since his right arm was crippled in the last encounter, he was learning to shoot left-handed.

Another Vaughan incident occurred on a train in Washington. In the fall of 1883, soon after the Northern Pacific Railroad was completed from St. Paul to the Pacific Northwest, Hank took a train ride to Idaho. On the return trip, when the train was near Sprague, he was dozing in his seat. Suddenly, two robbers entered the car, guns drawn, and ordered the passengers to put up their hands.

Hank did so with the others, but when the holdup men began collecting money, jewelry, and watches at the front of the car, he pulled his own gun and started blasting away. One robber was killed and the other made a hurried exit, jumping off the train. For his efforts, Hank was issued a lifetime pass by the grateful Northern Pacific Railroad.

Except for the killing of the deputy sheriff and the wounding of Sheriff Maddock when Vaughan was a youth, there is no record that he ever again shot a lawman, though he was arrested many times, usually for minor assaults and other mischief. Most of the officers who had to take him into custody for one thing or another respected his reputation, if not the man.

Umatilla County Deputy Sheriff Matt Taylor, uncle of famed sheriff Til Taylor, had to arrest Hank occasionally. His system, he told Fred Lockley of the *Oregon Journal,* was to wait until Hank had sobered up, then go out to Vaughan's home and arrest him. Hank always came along peacefully that way. One time he even invited the deputy to stay for dinner before they went to the jailhouse, and Matt accepted.

Another lawman who had no trouble with the fiery gunman was Adam Crossman, who was city marshal at Pendleton in 1881–82. When he first met Hank Vaughan, the marshal stood up to him, letting him know the rules he expected Hank to obey. Later that same day, Vaughan sought out Crossman, shook his hand, and bought him a new hat and walking stick. He told the marshal he liked his style, standing up to him that way, and said he would never give Adam any trouble whenever the lawman had to arrest him. And he never did.

When John Henry Durham was appointed as a new officer in Pendleton in 1889, Vaughan was among the first to congratulate him. He liked John and told him as long as Durham carried a badge he would never make trouble for him. Hank even went so far as to promise the new lawman help if he ever needed it.

Vaughan succumbed to the bliss of wedded life twice, as far as anyone knows. He was first married to a woman in Nevada, from whom he later separated. Believing her to be dead, he married a half-Indian widow lady named Robie, who had rights to a substantial acreage of good wheat farmland on the Umatilla Reservation. The new Mrs. Vaughan was the daughter of mountain man William Craig and a full-blood Nez Perce woman, who was herself a chief's daughter. Hank's marriage to the Widow Robie, however, proved to be unintentionally bigamous, for in 1888 the first Mrs. Vaughan showed up alive and wanting a divorce. Hank was happy to oblige.

Vaughan was a success as a wheat farmer, operating his grain business shrewdly, balancing costs against profits, and keeping his farm in the black. He was even able to enlarge the acreage by the purchase of an adjoining section of land, at $5.85 an acre, when the Umatilla Reservation was opened for public land sale.

Hank's marriage and farm responsibilities had not the slightest effect on his boisterous, often lawless life. On one occasion, he accompanied a saloonkeeper friend named Ed Horton to a land auction. During the bidding, Vaughan feigned a violent argument with the auctioneer and began shooting up the place. Though to others his anger appeared real, he was careful not to hit anyone.

It was later claimed that Horton and Hank—and maybe the auctioneer—had planned the disturbance. Horton wanted a piece of land, and when the bidding went beyond his price, he signaled to Hank to start shooting. The plan worked; the rival bidder ran off and Ed Horton's last bid was accepted by the auctioneer after things quieted down.

Hank Vaughan's end came in Pendleton on June 15, 1893 in an unexpected manner befitting his reckless life. The following two newspaper items give the details:

Pendleton *East Oregonian,* June 2, 1893

Hank Vaughn was out celebrating to some extent Tuesday afternoon. Mounted on his handsome sorrel horse, and wearing an air of bravado, he rode up and down the street to give a gratuitous "Wild West" show for the benefit of the Pendleton public.

At about 5:30 o'clock in the evening Hank put spurs to his steed and rode furiously down Main Street toward the depot, rider and horse nearly concealed in a cloud of dust. At a cross street just beyond the depot, in an attempt to make a sudden turn, the horse stumbled and fell, hurling Hank over its head into the gravel. Some of the spectators stated that the animal sprawled on top of its luckless rider.

It looked for a time that the man who appears to have nine lives and more too, so often has he been hurt and wounded, had at last been the victim of his own

Hank Vaughan took his last wild ride down Main Street in Pendleton.
(Umatilla County Historical Society)

> recklessness. He was taken to the Transfer House and Drs. Smith and Guyon summoned. From the effects of the hard fall he was for some time unconscious and it was hard to say how his injuries would terminate. Next morning, however, he had rallied in good shape and remarked almost cheerfully: "It's pretty hard to kill me off."
>
> He is hurt somewhat about the chest and may have a cracked rib. His eye is badly damaged and fearfully swollen, but it is thought he will not lose it. Hank's family were notified and arrived on the evening train from Athena to attend him.

Hank held his own for a number of days, but on June 20, 1893, the *East Oregonian* announced:

> HANK VAUGHN DEAD
>
> At 8 o'clock Thursday night death closed a colorful career. The operation on Hank Vaughn could not save the life that was almost extinct when it began, and in a few hours afterward, the quick disturbed breathing that was the sole evidence of the fast dimming vital spark ceased abruptly, and the soul of one of the most reckless beings who have given the "Wild West" its title was called to its Maker.
>
> Oh, Hank, that was a fateful ride, the last time you mounted your sorrel in the streets of Pendleton and sped with him like a tempest. Even his sure feet could not keep pace with your impulse, and you were plunged headlong upon the rocks.

Hank Vaughan's physicians noted that his body carried scars from thirteen bullet wounds.

CHAPTER 5

Street Showdowns and Other Misunderstandings

GUNFIGHTS IN OREGON'S early cattle towns and mining camps made a racket as often and in the same style as anywhere else in the West. Settling personal differences with guns happened more frequently in some places than others, of course, but such events took place in almost every settlement or district in old Oregon. In the state's wilder towns, where desperadoes, cutthroats, swindlers, and gamblers congregated, gun duels were common.

An old-timer from Canyon City once wrote: "Not a day or night passed which did not yield its full fruition of fights, wounds, or murders. The crack of the revolver was often heard above the merry notes of the violin. Street fights were frequent, and as no one knew when or where they would occur, everyone was on his guard against a random shot."

Thus, when The Dalles *Weekly Mountaineer* carried this short squib concerning a personal disagreement in Canyon City on March 23, 1866, it did not warrant much space: "John Grubb and C. Barr Smith fought. Grubb was shot in the groin as he was gouging out Smith's eye. Grubb died. Arrested, examined and acquitted, the homicide being considered justifiable."

Canyon City, where "the crack of the revolver was often heard above the merry notes of the violin." *(Grant County Historical Society)*

Most gunfights took place at short distances, often within the small space of a saloon. Many others happened outside, frequently at night. Seldom were they the planned, measured, slow-walk-down-the-street confrontations depicted in Western movies. Many times one of the participants did not even have a warning that he was about to be in a gunfight; the other man, pushed too far by drink or abuse, simply drew his iron and went to shooting. Some gun deaths were by ambush, and others resulted from one man being unarmed. Most shots fired in sudden, go-for-hell gunfights missed, even at close quarters. But not all of them.

The following are documented stories of gunfights and other showdowns in Oregon's early days. Some are brief, others are more detailed, and a few are even humorous in their way. Through them all is the smell of gunpowder, the

Many gunfights took place within the narrow confines of saloons such as this one at Denio. *(Harney County Historical Society)*

acid taste of fear, and the jarring awareness of possible death.

Not all quarrels involving guns took place in Oregon's wide-open cow towns or mining camps. We usually think of the Willamette Valley as a placid region of industrious, peace-loving pioneers, who found enough excitement in working their land. In general that was true, but some of the valley settlements also had their wild element—thieves, gunmen, and assorted n'er-do-wells who hung about the area saloons and gambling dens before moving on. And some of the "peace-loving" pioneers were themselves quite handy with a six-shooter.

Here are a few typical episodes that occurred in early Lane County, at the south end of the Willamette Valley.

In 1865 there was a dangerous and notorious character in Eugene City named Riley Deadmond, whose brother,

Henry, was hanged the year before in The Dalles for murder. Riley was a horse thief and bully, an unwelcome resident most Eugene City folks tried to stay clear of, for he was quick with a gun and had a history of assaults in Oregon and elsewhere.

On the night of February 10, 1866, Riley Deadmond was drinking hard in the Long Tom Saloon on Willamette Street. He was out on bond awaiting trial for a knife assault a couple of months earlier in the same saloon. He was in a mean mood and intimated that this would be his last night in town.

Riley began picking on a young boy who happened to be in the saloon. He ordered the youth to take a drink." When the boy refused, Deadmond tried to force liquor into his mouth. Stephen Gardner, the proprietor of the place, intervened and told Riley to leave the youngster alone. Enraged at his interference, Deadmond grabbed a stool and started toward Gardner, who retreated. Stephen Gardner knew that Riley always went armed, so before approaching the ruffian he had slipped a revolver into the back of his belt.

Stalking the cool-headed saloonkeeper, Deadmond dropped the stool and picked up a billiard cue, threatening to knock Gardner's head off. Gardner ordered him to lay off, but Riley still advanced, and when he was within six or eight feet of the saloon man, he suddenly put his hand in his coat. Believing Deadmond was going for a gun, Gardner fired. The bullet hit the badman in the chest, killing him almost instantly. A preliminary examination was held two days later, and Gardner was discharged on the grounds of self-defense.

The night of the shooting was, as Riley Deadmond had intimated, his last night in town, for the next day, after the coroner's inquest, his body was taken to the potter's field for burial—outside the city limits.

On the night of October 27, 1870, Robert Hadley was shot and killed in front of the St. Charles Hotel in Eugene City by David Felch, a night watchman. Less than a year previously, Hadley, a thief, attacked Felch while the latter was acting as watchman, firing a shot at him that missed. Felch had also fired, wounding Hadley in the shoulder.

Hadley was confined to his room for several weeks due to the injury. When he recovered, a charge of assault with intent to kill was brought against him. While he was under bond to appear before the circuit court at its next term, the two men met by chance on Willamette Street. As they approached each other, according to witnesses, Hadley suddenly put his hand into his coat as if to reach for a revolver. Felch quickly drew his gun and shot Hadley. Felch gave himself up to the sheriff at once, but upon examination was acquitted.

Not all Oregon gun battles grew out of personal insult or threats or drunken cussedness. At least one gunfight was over potatoes.

On October 23, 1882, A.J. Burnison and two other men, Barkdall and Snorff, were digging potatoes in a hop field. Burnison had grown the potatoes on land he rented from J.H. Brown. The primary crop was hops, and Burnison had put in the potatoes as a side crop. For some reason, Brown claimed that half the potatoes should be his; Burnison said not. So they were squabbling.

Anticipating trouble on this particular day, as farmer Brown had made caustic remarks and veiled threats, farmer Burnison took a revolver into the field with him. Brown arrived, also with a pistol strapped on, and began picking up and sacking the potatoes. He was warned by Burnison that he could not have any potatoes, and ordered to leave.

After an argument that lasted for some time, Brown apparently started away, then circled around Burnison two or three times, making threats and drawing nearer as each circuit was completed. Suddenly, Brown made a grab for his pistol, but Burnison beat him to the draw and fired. The first bullet missed. Brown crouched low, taking aim at Burnison. The potato grower fired again, this time hitting Brown and killing him. Burnison was acquitted at the November term of the circuit court.

The tough, dusty small eastern Oregon cow town of Burns was certainly no stranger to gunfights. One involved a colorful character named Jack Dalton, an adventurer who would later find fame and fortune far to the north in Alaska and the Yukon.

In the winter of 1883, Jack's name was not Dalton, it was Miller. A cowboy by trade, at that time Jack was running a small logging operation in the mountains north of Burns. On his crew was a cook named Matt Egan. Two

On this street in Burns Jack Miller (Dalton) killed Matt Egan in 1883.
(Harney County Historical Society)

or three days before Christmas, Jack fired Egan and hired in his place a buxom, middle-aged widow. The irate Egan took off for Burns and began drinking heavily. The more he drank the more he brooded.

A day or two after Christmas, Jack Miller came to town for supplies. According to witnesses, he had not been there long when he was accosted by Egan, who loudly berated him for pulling such a dirty trick. Miller, known for his quick temper and fighting ability, was cool and collected. He calmed his angry ex-employee by advising Matt to sleep it off and telling him that there was no reason they could not be friends. Temporarily appeased, Egan retreated for some further consideration at Broady Johnson's saloon. Jack went about his business of buying supplies.

According to the recollection of witness Maurice Fitzgerald, the truce between Egan and Miller was short-lived. Egan came out of Johnson's saloon and saw Jack's horse tied to a post across the street. Soon Jack came out of Smelser's Saloon and started walking toward his horse. Egan called out to Jack and motioned for him to come over. Miller walked toward Egan briskly, his arms swinging loosely by his sides.

Egan stood motionless until Jack was close, then suddenly drew a pearl-handled Smith and Wesson revolver from under his coat. As he did so, Jack Miller crouched and lunged at Matt. He grabbed Egan's wrist and forced it up as the gun went off, the bullet passing over Miller's shoulder.

Reaching with his other hand, Miller pulled his own gun, a Colt Bulldog, and raised it to fire. But Egan caught Jack's gun hand just as he shot, forcing it down so that the bullet went into the ground at Egan's feet.

The two men stood for a few seconds, each holding the other's gun hand. The shots had gathered a crowd, but no one moved to interfere. Both men were strong, but Jack slowly forced Egan's gun upward and brought his own in line with Egan's body. He quickly sent four bullets into his opponent's stomach. Egan slumped to the ground and died.

Flushed with the excitement of near death, and aware that several friends of Egan's were standing in the crowd, Miller picked up the dead man's revolver. Armed now with two guns, he strode back to Smelser's Saloon. None in the watching group made an effort to challenge Jack, and soon he quieted down. He turned Egan's gun over to Wash Smelser and rode back to his logging camp.

The small community of Burns buzzed with the news of Egan's death. Rumors were whispered of other shooting scrapes involving Jack Miller. Though the general opinion of witnesses was that Jack had been justified in shooting Egan, the law was not so sure.

Wallace W. Travillion, Baker County sheriff 1880–1884, trailed Jack Miller (Dalton) to Burns. *(Oregon State Sheriffs' Association)*

For a few days after the Egan killing, Jack was unmolested at his mountain camp. Soon more trouble headed his way, this time in the person of Sheriff Wallace Travillion of Baker County, to the north. He had a warrant for the arrest of Jack Miller on a charge of horse stealing. When a friend warned Miller of the sheriff's presence in Burns, Jack considered it an appropriate time to seek his fortune elsewhere. Avoiding the town, he struck southwest over the sage plains.

Jack made his way to San Francisco, and in 1884 he shipped out for Alaska. He signed aboard under a new name, one he would use for the rest of his life—Jack Dalton. Jack stayed in Alaska prospecting and exploring, and when the great Klondike gold rush was announced to the world in 1897, he blazed a route inland to the Yukon, suitable for driving cattle, sheep, and horses. His name was inscribed in history as the man behind the Dalton Trail.

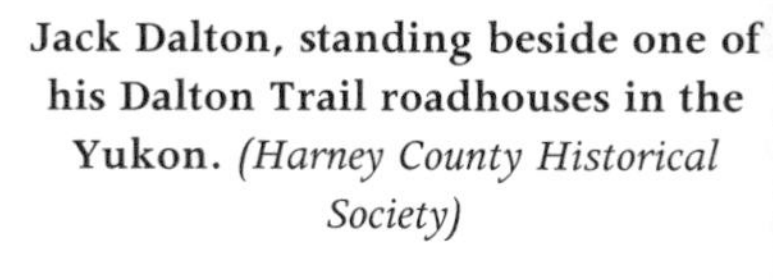

Jack Dalton, standing beside one of his Dalton Trail roadhouses in the Yukon. *(Harney County Historical Society)*

In 1884, Burns saw another gunfight on its dusty main street, and this one was rather unusual. John Bland and Horace Mace disagreed over some small matter and before long had carried their fight out to the street. There they drew their guns and started shooting at each other. When there were no more bullets in either gun, both of the badly wounded men laid down in the street, folded their arms over their chests like corpses in coffins, and died.

One of Burns' founders, Pete Stenger, had a gunfight with Rush Frazier in 1886 over Frazier's unwelcome advances toward Pete's wife. Frazier lost and was killed. Three years later Stenger was elected the first sheriff of Harney County when it was formed out of Grant County.

On September 8, 1888, a famed Harney Valley horse and cattle rancher named William H. Brown was killed in the Caldwell Saloon at Burns. Most agreed it was his own fault. Bill had been in an ugly mood that day in the saloon and had threatened William Page. Brown came at Page with a knife and knocked him down. From the floor, Page drew his gun and pumped four bullets into Bill Brown, thus rendering him a late Harney Valley horse and cattle rancher.

Another Burns saloon filled with gunsmoke on September 5, 1894. Two hard-nosed men from Prineville, Loren Parker and a big barkeep named Til Glaze, were in Burns to attend the Harney County Fair horse races. While in the Tex Saloon, they confronted a local man, Bud Howard, who had made an accusation against them earlier in the day. Guns were drawn by all three men. Howard killed Glaze and Parker killed Howard. In a trial verdict that was not popular with many Burns citizens, Parker was convicted of manslaughter and sentenced to the penitentiary for seven and a half years.

Fortunately, not all gun battles ended in death. Some

hurt no one at all. On the evening of June 26, 1880, the people who lived and worked along Front Street in Portland heard a lengthy series of gunshots in the street. Two former friends named Boles and White had gotten into an altercation in a Front Street saloon. Both were thrown out, and since each was armed, they decided to settle their dispute with revolvers.

They moved away from each other some distance, according to witnesses, and began shooting. The angry men emptied their guns at each other, amid curses. When the shots ended both were still standing. Then, to the amazement of onlookers, Boles and White turned without a further word and walked away in different directions—completely unscathed.

Long-standing feuds also sometimes ended in gunplay. In 1871, one of Oregon's most dramatic street confrontations happened in Roseburg. It could be called "The Case of the Gunfighting Editors."

Western newspaper editors of the nineteenth-century were often hard-drinking, rough-talking, tough-fighting men whose education came largely through experience. Journalism became highly personal, and they could get away with nearly anything in print. Libel law was in its infancy, and readers expected excitement from newspapers. Under such conditions, the writing of the unrefined journalists developed into free-swinging, colorful "reportage" in which caustic, ridiculing barbs were directed at opposing editors.

The seething cauldrons of editorial invective left readers gasping—or laughing—and highly entertained. Epithets such as: "willful slanderer," "villainous puppy," "notorious lying snake," "whiskey-filled pretender," and "old sausage cover" were hurled hotly between competing papers as each blasted the rascality of the other.

This warlike brand of writing became known as the "Oregon Style," because nowhere else was the sharp-tongued, biting manner of personal journalism carried to such extremes. Sometimes the newspaper feuds ended in bullets. In 1871, in the small Douglas County town of Roseburg, where the Oregon Style was deeply rooted, rival editors settled their differences in a spectacular gunfight on the main street. The battle had been a long time brewing.

Two brothers, Henry and Thomas Gale, established Roseburg's first newspaper, a weekly called the *Ensign,* in 1867. In 1870, a rival paper, the *Plaindealer,* made its appearance in Roseburg, steered by the acid pen of its editor and publisher, William Thompson. The Gales' *Ensign* was a Republican organ, revering Lincoln and President Grant, while Thompson's *Plaindealer* was staunchly Democratic.

The first three months after the *Plaindealer* hit the streets were relatively tame. But when Thompson mockingly called President Grant "Uriah Smith Grant," the *Ensign* was quick to respond. They said of the Thompson paper's style: "There is no wit in it, no sense, nothing but impotent malice."

Thompson retaliated by calling the *Ensign's* reporting policy "feeble lies about dead issues" and promised the *Plaindealer* readers that he would "report the truth of issues muddied by the *Ensign's* green hands."

Similar remarks continued in both papers for the rest of the year. The *Ensign* called the other paper a "lie sheet" and claimed it had a "blemished record for the truth." The *Plaindealer* announced that the Gale paper "has neither the patience to inquire nor sense to comprehend the truth of issues." To the *Ensign,* "our bigoted neighbor" was "an overgrown urchin." But, then, the Gales were "falsehood-dealing scoundrels."

Thomas Gale *(left)* and brother Henry, publishers of the Roseburg *Ensign,* fought a battle of words and bullets with rival William Thompson. *(Authors' collection)*

William Thompson, firebrand editor of the Roseburg *Plaindealer,* shot it out with the Gale brothers on June 11, 1871. He later led a vigilante gang in Prineville. *(Authors' collection)*

The feud escalated until the September 17, 1870 issue of the *Ensign* devoted twenty column-inches to insults directed at the *Plaindealer.* It said the Thompson paper was "driving ridiculously low into the cesspool of ignorance." According to the *Plaindealer,* the Gales had "brains of bootleather" and were "as sage as a squirt of tobacco juice."

By the end of 1870, the battle of abuse between the two newspapers had heated to a dangerous point. Long, rambling columns were devoted by each editor to the sharp personal denunciation of the other. The readers loved it, and some wrote letters to their favorite editor with scathing comments about the opposition paper. These letters were, of course, cheerfully published in the noble cause of free speech.

In June of 1871 William Thompson had become fed up with the constant and escalating attacks in the *Ensign.*

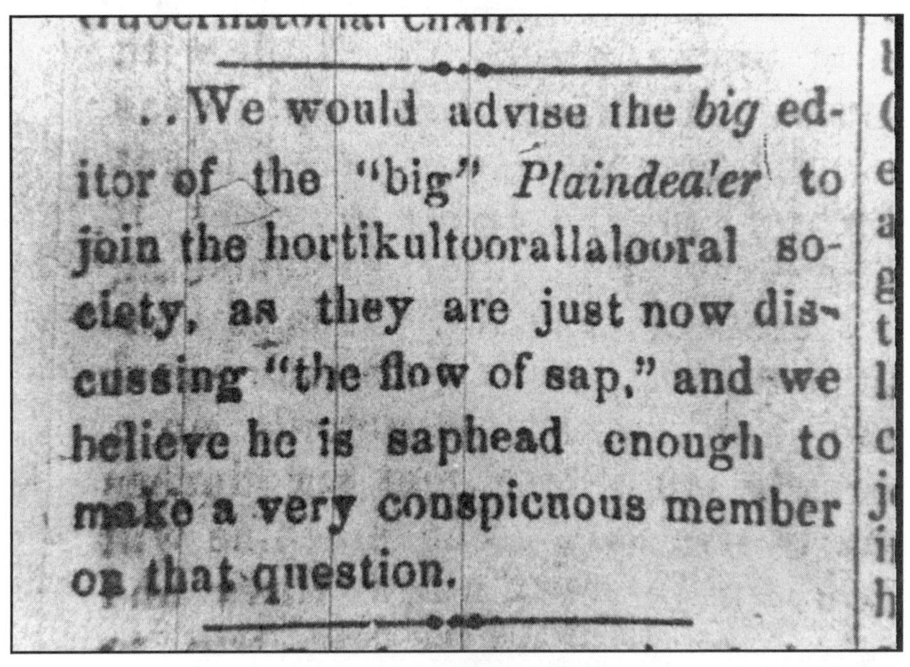

..We would advise the *big* editor of the "big" *Plaindealer* to join the hortikultooorallalooral society, as they are just now discussing "the flow of sap," and we believe he is saphead enough to make a very conspicnous member on that question.

Journalism in the "Oregon Style" led to traded insults in every edition of the *Ensign* and *Plaindealer.* *(Authors' collection)*

He told Thomas Gale personally that he would no longer submit to these insults. He was particularly incensed, therefore, when on June 10, the very next day after his talk with Gale, the *Ensign* ran several items blasting him. In a lengthy account of a recent stagecoach and rail trip the Gale brothers made to Eugene City, they made fun of Thompson's opposition to train travel. The article said the "Rosewater Pecksniff of the *Plaindealer*" should look into the improved cars of the quick mode of rail travel, and concluded: "The stupid fellow must wake up or move out of this country." Another item charged the *Plaindealer* with "unjustifiable extortion" for its advertising rates. Still another accused their "vanquished foe" of "raving."

That edition appeared on a Saturday, and later the same day Thompson ran into Thomas Gale at the Post Office. When an argument ensued, Gale put his hand into his pocket as if to draw out a pistol. Thompson immediately slapped Gale, grabbed his hand, and kicked him several times. That ended the first round, and the two angry editors parted.

Gale, it turned out, had been unarmed, but after leaving Thompson at the Post Office he ran to the *Ensign's* office, two blocks away. Then he and his brother armed themselves and went looking for Thompson, but nothing else happened that night.

At about ten o'clock the next morning Thompson and a friend named Virgil Conn were walking along Jackson Street when they saw the Gale brothers coming from the opposite direction. The Gales were armed. Though they later claimed the meeting was merely a chance encounter, it was suggested that they received reports from spies on the movements of William Thompson and were looking for a confrontation.

Jackson Street in Roseburg, shown here in 1870, was the scene of the bloody showdown between Thompson and the Gale brothers. *(Authors' collection)*

What happened next was observed by a number of eyewitnesses. According to reports, Henry Gale passed Thompson and Conn first without speaking. Thomas Gale, after passing Virgil Conn, said to Thompson: "You made a cowardly assault on me." Thompson said, "Well, what of it?" Henry Gale then told Thompson he should be ashamed for abusing a man so much smaller.

Henry then asked, "Why did you not jump on me?" Thompson replied, "If you are the one who does that part of the business, I will go after you the next time." Henry shouted some epithets. Thompson said he knew they were both armed and intended to attack him, but they were cowards and he was not afraid of them.

With that, Henry Gale struck Thompson on the left side of his face with a cane. Thompson kicked and punched Henry, but did not knock him down. Then Thomas Gale drew a pistol and shot Thompson at close range. The bullet entered at the corner of his vest pocket and passed through a number of papers before hitting him in the left side.

Thompson brought out his gun, a two-shot derringer, and fired into Thomas Gale's right side. He then turned on Henry Gale, beating him on the head several times with the gun. Thomas Gale hit Thompson on the head with a pistol. As Thompson turned toward Thomas, Henry Gale drew a four-shooter and shot Thompson in the neck. Thompson turned and received another bullet in the left shoulder.

Somehow, Thompson got off a shot at Henry, which hit him in the neck. At close quarters to Thompson, Henry pressed his pistol against the *Plaindealer's* editor's neck and fired. The bullet entered near the angle of the jaw on Thompson's left side and passed into his mouth. Thompson made an ineffectual attempt to speak and fell to the ground.

The fight was over. The Gales were taken to Dr. Hamilton's drugstore for treatment. Thompson was rushed to his home where he was treated by three physicians.

Miraculously, all three men survived the Jackson Street gunfight. On Monday, the sheriff arrested the Gale brothers for assault with intent to commit murder. They were never prosecuted.

Another feud that ended in gunsmoke took place in 1895 near the northeast Oregon town of Union. Kelsay Porter, a mild, small-scale farmer and stockman of good reputation, had for neighbors an uncouth, tough, bullying family named Maches, consisting of Ben, his wife, and Ben, Jr., a grown son. The Macheses were as bad in reputation as Porter was good. They had caused trouble for a number of Union County residents, and threats of shooting came easy to them. Feared most of all was Ben Maches, Jr., who had already served a stretch in prison and was known as a thug and bully around the district.

The main problem Kelsay had with them was that they

habitually used his field as a shortcut to their property. When passing through his gates, they always left the poles down, allowing Porter's stock to wander off. He informed them many times that they were not to trespass across his land, but they terrorized him with threats and displays of guns at every opportunity.

Finally, on January 1, 1896, Kelsay Porter had enough. Incensed because of the recent theft of a cow and a harness, he took his rifle and waited for his tormenters on a shed roof near his gate. Soon the three Macheses came through the gate in their buggy, and, as usual, left the poles on the ground. Kelsay hollered at them and heated words were exchanged. Kelsay would later state that young Ben fired first, but only the outcome is known for sure: Kelsay fired a total of eighteen shots, killing the father, the son, Mrs. Maches, and even their horse.

Porter turned himself in, and was tried and convicted of murder. Because of the reputation of the Maches family, a general feeling of sympathy and mercy for him prevailed in the county, yet the governor did not commute the sentence of death.

Kelsay was hanged by Sheriff J.F. Phy on the morning of November 19, 1897 before a crowd at the courthouse. As the solemn sheriff tightened the noose around the condemned man's neck, he said: "Porter, prepare to meet your Maker." He then sprung the trapdoor.

CHAPTER 6

"There's This Little Bank . . ."

Many Oregon outlaws were not particular about what they robbed, as long as there was a good chance to make a profit and an escape. Stagecoaches and solitary travelers were usually easy targets. Trains held more risk. But the chanciest endeavor of all was the bank robbery, and those who chose to conduct their nefarious business with banks were men of raw nerve or desperate circumstances.

Banks were tough. You had to go right into town to rob a bank, and generally the bank was located at the very center of the community. It was easy enough to go in and pull down on a teller or two and maybe a couple of customers—that was not the hard part. The difficulty was getting away. In the small wood-and-brick towns of early Oregon, there was an almost mystical sense of things going on. If something was happening in town, people knew it immediately and the word passed quickly.

Robbing a bank was hard to disguise: When one or two masked men with guns were sighted outside the front door of the bank, anyone could figure out what was happening inside. And townspeople were not happy when their bank was being robbed—their money was uninsured

The interior of this Sumpter bank was typical of Oregon banks in the 1890s.
(Baker County Historical Society)

in those days. As the hurried word passed that "The bank is being robbed!", armed men began appearing in doorways, windows, and on rooftops. More than a few Oregon bank robbers were shot down in a dusty street of an angry town, a money sack in one hand and a silenced gun in the other.

The Great Enterprise Bank Robbery

In 1891, Bill McCarty's ranching neighbors near Haines, in Baker County, thought of him only as a reclusive stockman who kept a low profile on his small cattle spread along the Powder River. He seemed to be gone much of the time, and he stayed to himself on his ranch, discouraging visitors when he was home. No one had anything bad to say about him, and they did not know he had other occupations. They did not know that their neighbor was

Tom McCarty, rustler and bank robber, led the McCarty Gang in numerous holdups in Oregon and the Northwest. *(Baker County Historical Society)*

also a train robber. And a stage robber. And a bank robber. And a rustler. And a business associate of Butch Cassidy. No, the ranchers around Haines did not know Bill McCarty very well at all.

McCarty's ranch, entered by a bridge over a placid bend in the Powder River, was a hideout for the McCarty Gang, which consisted at various times of: Bill McCarty; his brothers, Tom and George; Bill's sons, Eck and Fred (called by one rancher who knew him a "mean little weasel"); and an outlaw named Matt Warner. Matt's real name was Willard Erastus Christiansen. His sister, Teenie, was married to Tom McCarty.

Years before moving to eastern Oregon, Bill McCarty had hit the outlaw trail in Missouri and Minnesota. He took part in a number of robberies and did time in the Minnesota penitentiary for murder. Bill and Tom McCarty also operated for a time in Utah, stealing horses and cattle. Tom then went south to Arizona, where he and Matt Warner busied themselves in large-scale rustling. In the fall of 1887, Tom and Matt joined the notorious Butch Cassidy in a train robbery near Grand Junction, Colorado, and in 1889 Bill and Tom McCarty helped Butch hold up two banks in that state.

Outlaw Matt Warner *(right rear)* robbed banks with the McCartys and with Butch Cassidy's Wild Bunch. Shown in this 1902 photo standing with Warner is gunfighter Jack Egan *(left)*; seated are gunman Mid Nichols *(left)* and attorney Mark Braffett. *(Baker County Historical Society)*

Matt Warner's revolver and gunbelt. *(Baker County Historical Society)*

After some additional robberies, the McCartys decided to lie low for awhile. In late 1889 Bill purchased the small cattle ranch on the Powder River near Haines. There they lived quietly and anonymously, buying and raising stock and tending the ranch. George later bought property near Sumpter.

Tom McCarty and Matt Warner robbed a Butte, Montana gambling hall of $1,800 in the spring of 1890 and headed for a safe rest at Bill's Oregon ranch. To hide his identity in Oregon, Warner used the name Ras Lewis.

It was Bill's intent and fervent desire to maintain a peaceful haven for the family at the Haines ranch. To that end he asked that no one nearby be harmed and that no robberies be pulled in that district of Baker County. Brother Tom and brother-in-law Matt probably tried to accede to Bill's request, but the inner stirrings of some of the flour-sack brigade were difficult to ignore. Before long,

Interstate Highway 84 now cuts through the old McCarty ranch, near Haines.
(Authors' 1990 photo)

the gang conducted business at Summerville in adjacent Union County, at Sparta in eastern Baker County, and even in Baker City itself, just a few miles from the ranch. They also planned a bank robbery at Walla Walla but called it off. Next they robbed a Moscow, Idaho circus and got away only because lawmen hesitated to fire into the crowd.

Then came the bank at Enterprise.

In the fall of 1891, while Bill McCarty's neighbors thought him only a reclusive rancher, things were not going well for Bill. He was drinking heavily and was depressed and moody about recent financial losses. He blamed railroad companies, the government, and rich businessmen for his troubles. He was ready to strike back and made no further pretense to the others in the gang of wanting to keep low and safe.

The settlement of Enterprise, about ninety miles north by the wagon road from the McCarty spread, was the county seat of Wallowa County. The road wound around the western edge of the massive, snow-peaked Wallowa Mountains and into the cattle, wool, and wheat region of Enterprise and the Wallowa Valley. Servicing the banking needs of the area's farmers, ranchers, and townspeople was the handsome two-story brick Wallowa National Bank, located at the main intersection in Enterprise.

Nobody paid much attention to the three strangers who had been around town for a few days in early October 1891. Later it would be said that the men had been seen walking about town, keeping to themselves and camping in nearby woods. Thus, no one thought it odd when the three casually rode up to the Wallowa National Bank at one o'clock in the afternoon on October 8. Two of the men dismounted and entered the bank, while the third man remained on his horse, holding the reins of the other two horses.

The Wallowa National Bank of Enterprise was robbed by the McCarty Gang on October 8, 1891. *(Wallowa County Historical Society)*

It would have been frightening but helpful to the townspeople—and the Wallowa County sheriff, who leased office space above the bank—to know that the two men who sauntered into the bank were Bill McCarty and Matt Warner and that the man on the horse was Tom McCarty. The McCarty Gang was in town, and the first bank robbery in Enterprise was about to begin.

The bank cashier, W.R. Holmes, later related the event to the *Wallowa County Chieftain:*

> I had just returned from dinner, about one o'clock, and had entered the inside door to the bank office. When I reached the cashier's window, a man entered the front door, stepped up and asked if there was a deposit in the bank for Smith. I replied no. He again asked me if a deposit had been sent from Portland for Smith, and I again told him no. He said "Are you sure?" and I told him

> "Yes." Then without further conversation, the man produced a revolver, and with an oath ordered me to hand out the money. I began to back off, passing behind the glass windows of the office, and out of range of the robber's gun.
>
> About this time a second man jumped upon the metal wicket in front of the counter and, pointing his revolver at me, demanded that I stand where I was. A moment later he jumped into my office and was immediately followed by the first man. The men forced me to unlock the vault and hand out two sacks of silver and one of gold, containing $3,400 in all.

Meanwhile, out in front of the bank, Tom McCarty had pulled his gun and sat on his horse, keeping several people at bay with their hands up. George Gaily and L.O. Hoffman, operator of a private academy on the second floor of the bank building, looked out and had an unobstructed view of the commotion.

Just as the two inside robbers were coming out with the cashier in front of them, Tom took a shot at a man who attempted to enter. The shot startled the horses. As Matt Warner took the reins of his horse from Tom, the horse began bucking wildly. Matt later noted: "I never tried harder in my life to stick to a bronco, for if he throwed me he would throw me clear into jail."

The three bank robbers then spurred their horses south down the main street, shouting and yelling. A number of citizens had armed themselves by this time and were shooting at the fleeing outlaws, but none was hit.

Though the sheriff had been away from his office, soon a posse was gathered and began searching for the robbers' trail. There was only one road in or out of Enterprise and the posse pounded hard along it. The problem was that the McCarty Gang was not on the road at

The McCarty Gang outwitted the posse by escaping south over the massive Wallowa Range. *(Authors' 1990 photo)*

all. It was learned later from settlers in the district that the three men had ridden into the massive barrier range—the Wallowa Mountains—that separated the valley from the broad Powder River country and their ranch.

Realizing their only chance for a clean escape was by going over the Wallowa Mountains, the robbers headed straight for the 10,004-foot peak called Matterhorn. They fought their way through the cold and snow of what is now the Eagle Cap Wilderness area, finally emerged somewhere north of Baker City, and then proceeded west with their loot to Bill McCarty's place.

Because the McCarty Gang was not previously known in Wallowa County, it was not identified. In fact, no one was ever brought to trial for the Enterprise bank robbery. It was not even known until some years later, when Tom admitted it, that it had been the McCarty Gang who pulled the job.

After the Enterprise robbery, the McCartys' days were numbered. The following year, 1892, they robbed the Abrams, Snipes & Company Bank at Roslyn, Washington, and in 1893 they attempted to rob a bank in Delta, Colorado. That was a mistake.

On September 7, 1893, Bill, Tom, and Fred held up the Farmers and Merchants Bank in Delta. As they were riding away, a hardware store clerk named Simpson lifted and aimed his big Sharps .44-caliber rifle. He fired from over two hundred feet away. The heavy slug tore off the top of Bill McCarty's head. Tom kept riding, but Bill's son, Fred, stopped, dismounted, and leaned over the body of his father. Simpson fired again. Fred, the "mean little weasel," was struck in the back of the head by the bullet, which exited at the top of his forehead.

Though Tom McCarty escaped, the gang had been destroyed. Tom disappeared, forsook the outlaw trail, and died in self-imposed exile as a sheepherder. Brother George

Bill McCarty, dead in Delta, Colorado, 1893. *(Authors' collection)*

Fred McCarty, the "mean little weasel," was killed during the Delta robbery. *(Authors' collection)*

McCarty remained in Oregon, as did Bill's other son, Eck. Eck later killed a man in Baker City by plunging a corkscrew into his head, but got off on the grounds of self-defense. Both George and Eck died in obscurity. Matt Warner spent time in the Utah State Penitentiary from 1896 to 1900 for a killing. Upon his release he went straight, operated a saloon, and even worked for a time as a peace officer. He died in 1938.

The Fall and Rise of Dave Tucker

Shielding his eyes from the westering Oregon sun, the young man waited nervously on his horse. He and his two companions had a clear view down Third Street from their position on Schoolhouse Hill, a quarter-mile east of the bank, and they were watching for a signal.

The young man on the hill was David Tucker, and his companions were Cy Fitzhugh and Jim Brown. It was almost three o'clock on the afternoon of October 1, 1896, and they were getting ready to rob the Joseph bank.

The community of Joseph, nestled in the high Wallowa Valley of eastern Oregon, was a trading center for a large stock-growing region. Once the home of Chief Joseph and his band of Nez Perce, the "Valley-of-the-Winding-Waters" kept a tenuous hold on prosperity in the 1890s during the financial depression that had swept the entire country. The stockmen and farmers in the district had faith in their local economy, and they had faith in their bank, the First Bank of Joseph. It had never failed and it had never been robbed.

How Dave Tucker came to be waiting on that hill is not difficult to understand. Though he was a friendly, well-liked young man, he was easily led by others and already had been in trouble with the law. He later recalled that it

The town of Joseph was the site of a bloody bank robbery in 1896.
(Wallowa County Museum)

was considered a sort of game among the young men to put their brands on maverick cattle, and he joined in the game. The result was that Dave spent almost a year in prison in 1894 for cattle rustling.

Tucker was raised on a homestead east of the future site of Joseph. His schooling was sporadic, for schools were open only about three months out of the year. When Dave was old enough, he began herding sheep for Peter Beaudoin, a French-Canadian sheep rancher from Quebec, who was to become a major influence in his later life.

After the short stretch in the Salem penitentiary, Tucker held a variety of jobs on the Wallowa Valley sheep and cattle spreads, and he worked on the threshing crews harvesting vast acres of wheat. He was known to be a good hand for hard work. Then he met Cy Fitzhugh.

Cyrus Fitzhugh and Dave Tucker became acquainted

Dave Tucker rose from bank robber to bank officer. *(Oregon State Penitentiary photo)*

while they were working on a threshing crew in the summer of 1896. Fitzhugh was a stranger to the Joseph area, a tough drifter who regaled Tucker with tales of daring adventures, including robberies he committed around the West. He had been hanging around the Wallowa Valley for a few months, working on and off and telling people he was a prospector. But in fact, he told Tucker, he was nosing about for a good robbery opportunity.

Also on the threshing crew that summer was another drifter named Jim Brown. Together Fitzhugh and Brown approached Tucker with a proposition for easy money—they wanted him to help them rob the Joseph bank.

Tucker, who later said he was "soft and ignorant," had already been impressed by the persuasive, crafty Fitzhugh. After a number of discussions he agreed to join them.

The plan called for the assistance of two other local men: Ben Ownbey and a Joseph saloonkeeper named John Martin. They were to enter the bank as if on business. If things looked quiet, Ownbey and Martin would come out and give the signal. The trio on the hill would then ride down and pull the robbery. They planned to escape by riding south on Main Street out of town toward Wallowa Lake. Fresh horses would be staked in a grove of trees southeast of town. The gang would ride hard, lie low, and later meet with Ownbey and Martin to divide the spoils.

On Thursday, October 1, 1896, the boys were ready. A large wool deal had been consummated recently, and Fitzhugh figured there should be at least $8,000 in the bank. The fresh horses were waiting; Ownbey and Martin were en route to the bank; and on Schoolhouse Hill, Tucker, Fitzhugh, and Brown were waiting for the signal.

The mounted men watched their two confederates walk into the bank. In a few minutes Ownbey and Martin sauntered back out, slowly crossed the street, and leisurely returned to the bank and went inside. That was the signal. The raid was on. The three men on the hill rode down Third Street and tied their horses to a wagon that stood in front of Cole's blacksmith shop near the bank.

Running alongside the bank toward the front door, the robbers pulled masks over their faces. Armed with a shotgun, Fitzhugh entered first, Brown close on his heels. Tucker remained outside the front door with his gun drawn to keep people away. Almost immediately, J.A. Hooper, a townsman who was walking across from the bank, saw the armed, masked men enter and he yelled: "Those men are going to hold up the bank." Tucker leveled

The First Bank of Joseph. During the robbery, Tucker stood guard on the front steps. His fellow robber, Jim Brown, died in the street near the right side of the photo. *(Wallowa County Museum)*

his gun at Hooper and ordered him to come across the street. The frightened man approached with his hands raised.

Inside the bank, Fitzhugh announced the holdup and quickly lined up the employees and customers, covering them with his shotgun. Martin and Ownbey, posing as customers, were kept at bay with the others so that their connection would not be known. Cashier J.D. McCully was forced to gather the money and put it in a bag held by Jim Brown.

Meanwhile, the situation outside was heating up. Alex Donnelly and W.H. Burton, who were in a building across from the bank, heard Hooper yell something about the bank being robbed. Seeing a masked gunman standing outside the front door, Donnelly and Burton then ran out the back of their building and separated. Donnelly ran down Main Street giving the alarm while Burton hurried to the nearby Third Street house of Fred Wagner.

Upon learning of the robbery in progress, twenty-four-year-old Fred Wagner loaded his Winchester .45-75 rifle and crept cautiously outside, where he had a view to the front of the bank, a half-block away.

At the same time, businessman Fred McCully was en route to the bank to deposit money. Alex Donnelly swept past him, blurting a warning that the bank was being held up, but thinking it was a joke, McCully went on. When he reached the corner bank entrance and ran smack into the masked gunman standing guard, McCully realized that Donnelly had been serious. He was ushered inside and made to contribute to the gang's shotgun withdrawal.

The small town was quickly becoming aware of the robbery, and the men inside were taking too long. Tucker was doing the best he could, but he began to see furtive figures darting here and there among buildings, and some of the braver townspeople were watching from out in the open. Tucker warned several away with his gun, then hollered inside to Fitzhugh and Brown to hurry up.

Finally, the two robbers emerged from the bank. Brown held the bag containing $2,000, and Fitzhugh still had control of the captives, prodding them outside with his shotgun. After releasing the bank customers near the front door, Brown, Fitzhugh, and Tucker attempted their getaway, running along the side of the bank toward their horses.

Once the hostages were in the clear, Fred Wagner went into action. He had positioned himself west of the bank on Third Street with his big .45-75, and now he took a bead on the escaping robbers. His first shot missed. Dave Tucker returned fire, the bullet striking close to Wagner. Wagner aimed at the man with the money bag, Jim Brown, and

Fred Wagner, the brave resident who shot it out with the Joseph bank robbers. *(Wallowa County Museum)*

fired again. This time his aim was true, and Brown was drilled through the chest. He fell dead in the street on top of the money bag.

Other townsmen with rifles were also shooting at the fleeing bank robbers from concealed positions. In a hail of bullets, Fitzhugh ran to Brown, rolled the dead outlaw over, grabbed up the money bag, and continued his sprint for the horses.

Meanwhile, Dave Tucker was also trying to get to the wagon where the horses were tied. As he reached the rear corner of the bank, another shot from Fred Wagner struck Tucker's gun hand, tearing off his trigger finger and part of his thumb. He turned abruptly into the alley at the back of the bank and was almost immediately shot again by Alex Donnelly. After running up Main Street shouting the alarm, Donnelly had grabbed a shotgun and gone into the bank through a rear door. As Tucker came past the alley door, Donnelly fired. Several of the buckshot hit Tucker in the side, but he managed to keep running some distance. He was captured by H.P. Throe a couple of blocks away.

The only robber to reach the horses was Cy Fitzhugh, who had the money bag. He leapt on his horse amidst flying bullets and galloped south out of town toward the low hills east of nearby Wallowa Lake. He was never caught, and his fate remains unknown.

After Dave Tucker was shot twice and captured, he was taken to Dr. Barnard's office for treatment. Soon he was hauled into court for a preliminary hearing, where he pled guilty to the bank robbery charge and was sentenced to seven years in the Oregon State Penitentiary at Salem.

It was later learned that Ben Ownbey had been involved in the robbery. Upon being charged, he, too, pled

Cy Fitzhugh was last seen in this swale escaping with the gold from the Joseph bank. *(Authors' 1990 photo)*

guilty and was sentenced to a five-year prison term. John Martin was also tried but freed due to a lack of evidence.

Dave Tucker's prison sentence for robbing the First Bank of Joseph was not the end of this story.

The twenty-five-year-old bank robber served over four years of his sentence, working in the prison shops and mail office. He was a model prisoner and was released in 1901. Upon his release Dave returned to the Wallowa Valley to face his parents and friends and to try to build a new life.

Fortunately, Pete Beaudoin, the kindly French-Canadian sheep rancher, put Tucker to work as a herder and camp tender. He worked for Beaudoin for several years and in 1905, with a band of lambs bought from his employer, Dave went on his own in the sheep business.

Kindly rancher Pete Beaudoin *(left)* gave Dave Tucker *(right)* a job after his release from prison. The boy *(center)* is Beaudoin's son. *(Wallowa County Museum)*

Soon he acquired land and over the years accumulated 1,200 acres. He also bought cattle and raised beef as well as sheep.

In 1906 Dave married a local girl, Minnie Proebstel, and they had three children. With his ranch and small family, the rehabilitated robber was on his way to a successful life. As the years passed, Tucker became one of the largest and most respected stockmen in the county. He was made head of the Wallowa Valley Improvement District, and was a director of the school district.

But he remained painfully aware of his debt to those he had wronged, and he felt he had never fully atoned for his part in the Joseph bank robbery. As he became prosperous, he helped many people in Joseph and the Wallowa Valley with gifts and loans of money. He was well-liked and trusted, a responsible leading citizen of the area.

The former First Bank of Joseph now houses the Wallowa County Museum.
(Authors' 1990 photo)

Finally, in 1928, twenty-seven years after his release from prison, Dave Tucker was elected vice-president of the former First Bank of Joseph, by then renamed the Joseph State Bank. He had traveled a long trail from that day in October 1896, when he stood with mask and gun at the intersection of Third and Main. Dave Tucker had become an officer of the same bank he robbed.

CHAPTER 7

VIGILANTE DAYS

IN OREGON'S WILD EARLY DAYS, from the 1860s to the 1880s, properly constituted law officers and courts were scarce or nonexistent in some districts, particularly in the vast mountain and sage plains country of eastern Oregon. Justice was often slow or lacking entirely in certain areas, and some murderers, robbers, and rustlers went unpunished. As a result, a sort of do-it-yourself law enforcement came into being: vigilantes.

Made up of serious-minded, justice-seeking members of the mining and ranching communities, the vigilantes saw themselves as avenging angels, defending their families and land against the scourge of unrestrained outlaws. Between 1863 and 1865, there were thirty-two documented cases of outlaws hanged by vigilantes along the routes to Oregon and Idaho mines. Many oaks, pines, and junipers were decorated with the dangling bodies of retired desperadoes.

In 1864, the end of the notorious Henry Plummer gang came by vigilante ropes. Plummer, the outlaw sheriff of the Bannock City and Virginia City districts in what was then Idaho Territory, had sent his murdering rustlers and cutthroats into eastern Oregon on many forays. On January 10, 1864, he and those in his employ were strung up in Bannock by the vigilantes. Four days later Boone Helm and four other members of the Plummer gang dangled from ropes in a barn at Virginia City.

Also in that year, a horse thief named John Weatherly was hanged by vigilantes in a little valley on the Powder River, near the present town of North Powder, Oregon. The stern message went out to other rustlers, and the district, now known as Thief Valley, remained free from stock theft for years.

Vigilante committees sprouted in many areas of Oregon during those turbulent years, and they were controversial—supported by some, condemned by others. Even the newspapers were split on the subject. The Roseburg *Umpqua Ensign* acknowledged the existence of a local vigilante committee in 1871, but decried its presence. "It is entirely wrong," opined the editor, "and should be frowned down by every law abiding man in our country." But in 1880, in the same community, the *Douglas Independent* advocated "a little hemp diet" for stage robbers operating in southern Oregon.

Not always were the culprits hanged when caught by the vigilantes. Sometimes they were simply run out of town. In the fall of 1884, Umatilla County ranchers decided to end a long series of horse and cattle thefts by organizing a committee to snatch up the suspected rustlers and turn them over to the law at Pendleton.

The accounts differ as to numbers, but somewhere between a dozen and fifteen evil-doers were rounded up in November and brought to town, where they were turned over to Deputy Sheriff J.B. Eddy. There were too many culprits for the small jail, so Deputy Eddy assigned two men to guard them in the county courthouse. The angry cattlemen stayed in town all through the day, concerned that their prisoners would either escape or be released. More cowmen drifted into town and jammed the Pendleton saloons. Soon talk of lynching spread through the streets. By evening about 300 ranchers and sympathizers met and listened to speakers call for law and order, while others demanded more direct action.

Then a former Umatilla sheriff, Ad Nye, was sent by the vigilantes to see Deputy Eddy. Nye told him that the prisoners would be given a chance to leave town on the next train, lest their lives be in danger. Most of the prisoners were happy to oblige, sensing their doom at the ends of vigilante ropes. One by one, the suspects boarded the morning eastbound, and a few were allowed to wait until that evening when the westbound train came through.

Oliver Stanley sought refuge from vigilantes in his Pilot Rock blacksmith shop *(behind white tent)*, circa 1880. *(Umatilla County Historical Society)*

One man, however, a suspected cattle thief named Oliver H. Stanley, bolted from the crowd, jumped on a nearby horse, and rode off into the night. Stanley operated a blacksmith shop in Pilot Rock, fifteen miles to the south. The next day the cattlemen received word that he had gone home and was barricaded inside his shop.

He did not remain in his fort for long. Learning that the vigilantes were coming to get him, he sent word to the Pilot Rock constable that he would give himself up if the law would escort him safely to the proper authorities in Pendleton. The constable agreed and with another man took Stanley into custody and began the trip.

At dusk the party was about seven miles out of Pilot Rock when a large band of vigilantes appeared from the north. The outnumbered constable made no resistance when the masked riders ordered him and his helper to put their hands up. Seeing that his end was near, Stanley kicked up his horse and bolted away. Several vigilantes fired a volley of shots at him, and he fell dead from his horse.

No one was ever arrested or brought to trial for Stanley's murder. At the inquest the coroner's jury ruled that O.H. Stanley "came to his death by wounds received from a posse of men unknown to the jury." Local rustling stopped for quite some time.

There were other occasions when vigilantes brazenly took prisoners away from proper legal authorities. On November 29, 1885, rustler George Keach was forcibly taken from a Umatilla County officer named Adams by masked riders. A scaffold was hastily constructed of fence rails and Keach was hanged. In the early hours of July 7, 1887, murderer Oscar Kelty was broken out of the Polk County jail at Dallas and strung up on an oak tree adjacent to the courthouse. The masked group of vigilantes that hanged him, some thirty strong, was led by one Abraham Blackburn, who was later tried and acquitted for lack of evidence. The oak hanging tree can still be seen on the southeast side of the Polk County courthouse.

Another case of jailbreaking by vigilantes came as late as 1894. It occurred in Lakeview at one o'clock on the morning of August 20. The prisoner, W.S. Thompson, was in jail on charges of drawing a gun on several people. An uncouth, dangerous bully, Thompson had run amok in Lake County for some time. He regularly assaulted his wife and children, as well as other people, and was quick to point a gun at anyone who got in his way. He was also known to kill horses and cattle when he was in a mean mood.

Frustrated with a slow judicial process, masked men forced their way into the jail and made the lone night-jailer open Thompson's cell. Then they dragged the prisoner to the courthouse steps, threw a rope over a porch beam, and cured Thompson of his antisocial behavior permanently.

One of the main problems law-abiding citizens found with vigilante law was that there was no procedure for true, accurate determination of guilt, as required in legal courts. Such inconveniences as proper evidence, competent testimony, and the right to a defense, as spelled out in the United States Constitution, were not a part of vigilante law enforcement. That they most often hanged the actual culprit there is no doubt. But not always. For example, there was the tragic case of John Hawk.

A young stockman named John Hawk wrested a meager living from a small cattle ranch on Prairie Creek in Wallowa County. In 1879 the cattlemen in the high Wallowa country shared thousands of acres of open range, depending upon the honesty of their neighbors to keep the right brands on the right animals.

The hanging tree at Dallas in 1900. *(Polk County Historical Society)*

The hanging tree at Dallas in 1994. *(Authors' photo)*

It was a fact of open-range life, however, that some cattle were lost to roving rustlers, who cut out what they wanted and drove them east across the Snake River into Idaho, or north to Washington. As time went on, it became obvious to a number of the Wallowa Valley ranchers that young, reclusive John Hawk was steadily increasing the size of his once modest herd. Since Hawk was known to have no means of income other than his ranch, they figured he must be stealing cattle and putting his brand on them. Suspicion grew until by the spring of 1881 it was a common opinion among Hawk's neighbors that he was nothing but a vile, low-down cattle rustler.

Through the spring and early summer branding time Hawk was carefully watched, but nothing could be proved that would satisfy a court. The ranchers wanted something done before they lost more cattle. Finally, a decision was reached: they would kill him. A committee of vigilantes was chosen to carry out the deed, and it was not long before they had a plan.

In the early fall of 1881, John Hawk was approached by one of the vigilantes and offered a job. John accepted, not knowing he was a marked man. The job was to haul a wagon load of shingles sixteen miles from Joseph to the settlement of Lostine. The plan called for an ambush along the way, but it was thwarted when John picked up his mother and two friends, Mr. and Mrs. Sam Adams, and took them with him to Lostine. The disappointed vigilantes watched from hidden places as the wagon rolled by unharmed.

Hawk dropped the women off to visit a friend while he and Sam Adams delivered the shingles. After disposing of his load, John discovered that he would need to have some horseshoeing done before returning to Joseph. By the time the blacksmith finished it was nightfall, so Hawk and

Adams decided to camp overnight in a small tent on the nearby Lostine River, then pick up the women in the morning and head back to Joseph. It was just the opportunity the vigilantes were waiting for. They wanted Hawk, and would have him, even if his friend had to be killed, too.

Sam Adams would later relate that sometime during the night, after the two men were in their beds, he was awakened first by a single shot, then a fusillade of shots outside the tent. Adams quickly ducked under the bottom of the tent and scurried uninjured into some bushes, where he shivered through the night. He was lucky, for had he not bolted at the first shot, he surely would have been struck by those that followed.

John Hawk was not so lucky—he was dead. It was thought that one of the vigilantes had crept up to the tent, discovered which side of the tent Hawk was on by the voices inside, and then signaled to the others, who commenced firing. Hawk was twenty-nine years old and left a widow and two children. The murderers were never caught.

There was one small problem with this episode of vigilante justice—John Hawk was not guilty of anything. If the ranchers had checked into the matter more carefully, perhaps by asking John where he got his new cattle, they would have learned that the animals belonged to a Prairie Creek friend and neighbor, Fred Proebstel.

Proebstel had gone through a difficult divorce and wanted to keep certain of his assets hidden from his wife. It was arranged with John Hawk that Fred would buy cattle and put them on John's land, under John's brand, with the understanding that they really belonged to Proebstel. That arrangement went on for a couple of years, during which time the suspicions of certain area ranchers were aroused against John Hawk. Seeing his herd increase from about 50 to over 300 head, without a proper investigation they decided he was a cattle rustler. They were wrong.

Jim Blakley and the Prineville Vigilantes

One of the most dramatic accounts of lawless vigilante rule in Oregon is the story of what happened in Prineville during the early 1880s. It is also the tale of a young cattleman's courageous efforts to stop the fearsome, power-hungry, masked nightriders of central Oregon.

Crook County was not yet formed in 1882; the vast area around Prineville that would become Crook County was then part of enormous Wasco County. The county seat and sheriff's office were located at The Dalles, 130 miles to

Prineville, on the high-desert of central Oregon, was plagued by vigilantes in the early 1880s. *(Bowman Museum Collection)*

the north. The only law in the rough, dusty cow town of Prineville was a town marshal, W.C. Foren, and a deputy sheriff named John Luckey. They enforced the law in a district larger than several eastern states.

At that time Prineville was the center of one of the state's principal stock-growing regions. Disgruntled over incidents of rustling and fearful of Indian attacks from high-desert raiders, a number of outlying ranchers formed a loose-knit stockman's protective association in the winter of 1881-82. Their aim was to deal quickly and harshly with those who caused trouble, be they Indian or white. The leader was a quick-tempered, outspoken firebrand who had been an Indian fighter and pioneer newspaper editor. He was William Thompson, the same man who had shot it out with rival editors on the streets of Roseburg in 1871. When he established himself in the cattle business near Prineville in the early '80s, Thompson still carried a ball in his neck from the 1871 gunfight.

One of the first Prineville residents to oppose the vigilantes was a twenty-nine-year-old cowman named Jim Blakely, who refused to associate himself with the Thompson "protective" group and with their tough talk of quick action and gun law. The son of ox-team pioneers who crossed the plains to Oregon in 1846, James M. Blakely was born in the Willamette Valley settlement of Brownsville in 1852, and by age thirteen he was in the saddle as a seasoned cowhand and a crack shot with revolver or rifle.

By early 1882 Jim had acquired his own ranch near Prineville and had 1,500-head of stock. He earned a reputation as an honest, clear-thinking rancher who did not cause trouble but did not run from it.

The first instance of vigilante action by Thompson's protective group came in March 1882. On the fifteenth of that month, rancher A.H. Crooks and his son-in-law,

James M. Blakely was the first elected sheriff of Crook County. *(Oregon State Sheriffs' Association)*

Stephen Jory, friends of William Thompson, were killed by a neighbor named Lucius Langdon over a property line dispute.

William Thompson's vigilantes, including Charley Long, the man who shot it out with Hank Vaughan in a Prineville saloon, went looking for the suspected killer. Thompson and his men glimpsed Langdon at a line cabin on Mill Creek, but in the dark their quarry got away.

Because Deputy John Luckey was unavailable the next day, a number of Prineville citizens persuaded Jim Blakely to head another posse to look for Lucius Langdon, doubtless with the hope of having the fugitive arrive in Prineville alive. Blakely agreed, and at dusk his small party reached the Langdon ranch. When they were about 200 yards from the house, a dog barked and the men saw

Langdon mount a horse and start away. Blakely called out to him and Langdon stopped, wheeled around, and rode back to him, relieved that it was Jim Blakely who had caught him. Blakely and his men took their captive to the house, where Mrs. Langdon fixed them supper. Then they headed to Prineville. Around two o'clock in the morning, Blakely woke Deputy Luckey and turned over the captured murder suspect.

There was no regular jail in Prineville in those days, so Luckey took Langdon and a man named W.H. Harrison, who was arrested as an accomplice, to the Jackson Hotel for safekeeping until he could transport them to The Dalles. In addition to himself, Luckey had two men at the hotel as guards.

At about five o'clock in the morning Langdon was sleeping on a lounge in the hotel lobby and Harrison was

Prineville's Jackson Hotel, where vigilantes killed one man and dragged out another to be hanged. *(Bowman Museum Collection)*

awake sitting by the stove. Deputy Luckey later claimed that suddenly the front door burst open and a number of masked men rushed into the room. They overpowered and blindfolded the guards, then shot Lucius Langdon to death. The vigilantes then grabbed Harrison and took him outside, where Deputy Luckey and the others could hear him begging for his life.

While the frightened townspeople watched and listened from behind curtains on that dark morning, the mob of vigilantes put a rope around Harrison's neck, attached the other end to the saddle horn of a mounted masked rider, and dragged him the length of the main street to the bridge over Crooked River at the west edge of Prineville. He was hanged from a crossbeam under the bridge.

The murders of Langdon and Harrison were the first

Vigilantes hanged W.H. Harrison from this Prineville bridge in March 1882.
(Bowman Museum Collection)

deaths attributed to William Thompson's vigilantes, but not the last. Though they claimed their protective association was to make the county safe from outlaws and rustlers, no outlaws were ever captured by them. William Thompson essentially ran central Oregon after the March 1882 murders, and few people dared to oppose the powerful, ruthless vigilante leader. Some area residents who did criticize him mysteriously received skull and crossbones notes warning them to keep quiet.

The vigilantes next began attempting control of the open range by issuing orders to cattlemen that permits would have to be requested of the association before anyone could ride the range. Jim Blakely was the first to openly defy Thompson's gang. He sent back his own orders, saying that he was born in the Oregon country and "I'll be damned if anyone is going to tell me when I can go out after my own stock." He bought two new .41 Colt revolvers and three .32 Smith and Wessons for his riders. He and his men were not bothered by the vigilantes.

Jim Blakely's .41 Colt. *(Oregon State Sheriffs' Association)*

After months of intimidation, the vigilantes killed again. Rancher Al Schwartz had sided with Jim Blakely, openly expressing his opinions about the nightriders. On the night of December 24, 1882, while Schwartz was playing cards at the Burmeister Saloon, he was shot twice in the head by a masked vigilante who aimed through a window.

Later on that same Christmas Eve, two young cowboys from the Schwartz ranch, Sid Huston and Charley Luster, were murdered by masked riders. Huston and Luster had been lured to the cabin of W.C. Barnes, located on the road about a mile east of Prineville, where they were attacked by vigilantes. The young men were overpowered and taken across the road, where they were both strung up on a large juniper tree. They were then shot in the backs of their heads.

Jim Blakely was notified the next morning and he rode out to recover the bodies. Through a newspaper item, the vigilantes took credit for the Schwartz, Huston, and Luster

On this knoll east of Prineville, vigilantes strung up Huston and Luster on Christmas Eve 1882. *(Authors' photo)*

killings, stating that the three had been part of a stock-theft ring. But Blakely and others knew it was not true. Blakely also knew that Schwartz had been outspoken in his denouncement of the vigilantes.

The vigilante killings continued. Soon after the Christmas Eve murders, a rancher named Steve Staats, who had also been openly critical of Thompson's gang of terrorists, had the top of his head blown off near Stearns Butte. Following that murder, a Prineville rancher named Shorty Davis, a good citizen and a mild genteel fellow who opposed the vigilantes, suddenly disappeared. His body was never found.

A few months later in March 1883, vigilante J.M. Barnes killed unarmed Mike Morgan in Burmeister's Saloon. In December, William Thompson himself killed Mike's brother, Frank Morgan, by shooting him in the back of the head in Kelly's Saloon. There was no indication that the men were rustlers, but in neither case were the killers charged. *Oregonian* editor Harvey Scott stated publicly that if Thompson wanted any man dead, the man was as good as buried.

The Morgan murders finally incensed the community. Prior to the winter of 1883-84, Jim Blakely, Sam Smith, and John Combs had been the only men left alive of the outspoken anti-Thompson faction. They were joined now by a number of others. A secret meeting was called one night at the Stuart and Pett flour mill near Prineville. There the men organized as a group and vowed to fight Thompson's riders. They called themselves the Citizens Protective Union, but soon they were dubbed the "Moonshiners" because they kept watch and patrolled at night when the masked terrorists rode. Their ranks quickly increased to about eighty respected, established residents of the Prineville district who were bent on ending the bloody dictatorship of William Thompson.

In early 1884, not long after the formation of the Moonshiners, vigilante Gus Winckler let it be known that if Jim Blakely did not watch his step, he would be next on The Hill, referring to the cemetery. When Blakely heard the threat third-hand, he strapped on his Colt .41 and went looking for Winckler.

He spotted the vigilante talking to another man near the Jackson Hotel. As Blakely approached, Winckler went into the hotel and out the back door to the outhouse. Blakely followed and ordered him to come out. The frightened nightrider came out with his hands raised. Blakely marched Winckler out to the street and loudly announced that if the vigilante was not on the next stage out of town, he would not get out of Prineville alive. The chagrined Gus Winckler left on the next coach and never returned.

By the spring of 1884, the vigilantes were facing a growing, open opposition from Prineville citizens, many of whom were Moonshiners, ready to stop the two-year control by Thompson's gang. The long awaited showdown came on a spring day when Jim Blakely and the others decided to end it once and for all.

Vigilante George Barnes had made the mistake of declaring openly in a Prineville saloon that the vigilantes would destroy the Moonshiners. Upon receiving news of the threat, Blakely gathered his men. The vigilantes were holding a mass meeting at their headquarters in the Til Glaze Saloon, and it was there that the courageous young cowman led his Moonshiners. Vigilante lookouts, peering through the saloon windows, saw eighty armed, determined men riding slowly and calmly up the main street. The massive body halted in a semicircle directly in

Prineville's Main Street, where Blakely and the Moonshiners marched on the vigilantes in the Til Glaze Saloon *(building with round roof, left).* *(Authors' collection)*

front of the saloon. Townspeople watched from behind wagons, doors, and curtains to see how it would end.

Jim Blakely, his .41 Colt holstered at his side, called to the men in the saloon, challenging them to come outside and have it out right then and there. The vigilantes made no response and stayed where they were. In that instant, and without a shot fired, public fear turned to scorn and the grip of the vigilante gang was broken.

On June 2, 1884, the first election was held in Crook County, and Jim Blakely was elected sheriff. William Thompson quickly sold his ranch, sleeping in a barn with his gun close at hand until the deal was completed. He then fled to California where he started a newspaper. The rule of the vigilantes in central Oregon was over.

James Blakely served two terms as sheriff of Crook

County. In 1888 he moved to Wallowa County, where in 1904 he was elected sheriff and again served two terms. The man who ran the vigilantes out of Crook County passed away peacefully on January 23, 1953 at almost 101 years of age.

CHAPTER 8

Bars, Stripes, and the Brickyard

THE FIRST OREGON JAIL was built in April 1845. It was a sturdy two-story, twenty-foot-square log blockhouse constructed in Oregon City by an act of the Provisional Government "for the imprisonment of all criminals in Oregon." The jail was accessible only by an outside staircase leading up to the second level, in the middle of which was a hole three feet square. The prisoner was lowered through the hole into the ground-floor room, and a guard remained on duty in the upper room ready to club any head that poked up from below.

This curious arrangement lasted only a little more than a year because on the night of August 18, 1846, someone burned the jail to the ground. The culprit was never caught, even with the posting of a $100 reward. There would not have been a place to keep him anyway, for after the destruction of the jail at Oregon City, there was no other governmental prison built for more than ten years.

In the years before and after the short-lived Oregon City jail, the restraint of prisoners prior to trial and upon conviction was left to the imagination of the local authorities. On some occasions, in good weather, a

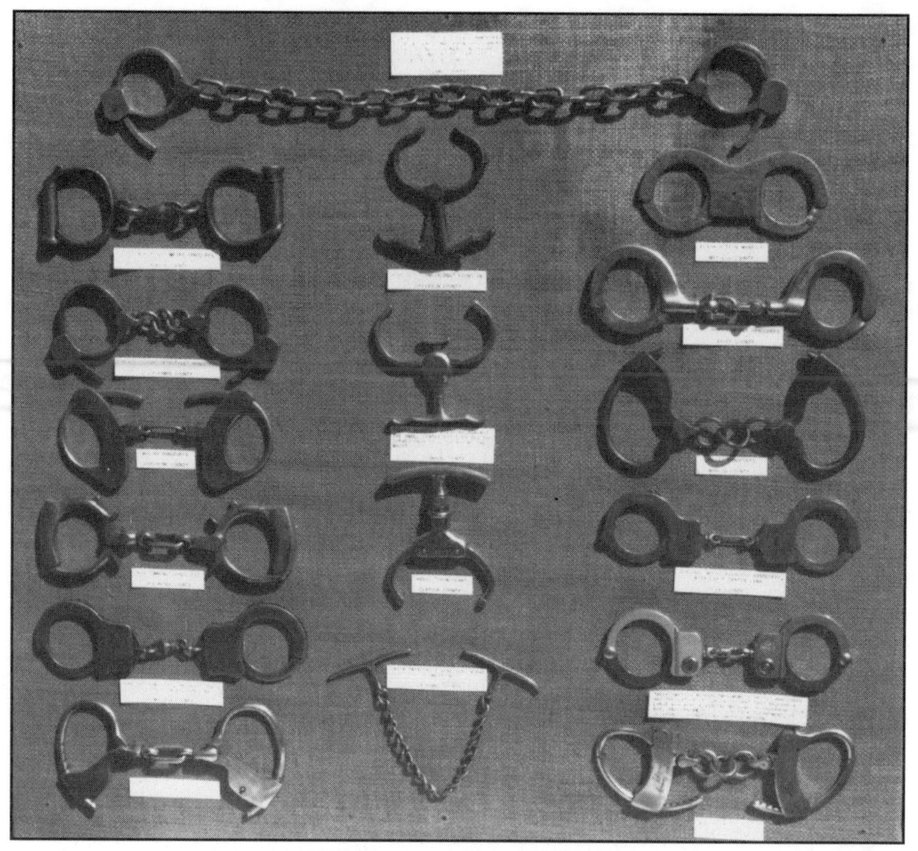

Display of old-style restraints used by Oregon lawmen.
(Oregon State Sheriffs' Association)

lawbreaker was simply chained to a tree or a log to be fed and watched over by a guard hired for the purpose.

In most cases, however, a convict was bid out to a local farmer or other workman, who received a contracted sum for his keeping. The aim was to maintain the prisoner at hard labor for the duration of his sentence, but sometimes he would be kept in chains, locked away in a spare room or outbuilding for his term, or until he escaped. Escapes were frequent and records show that few contracted prisoners ever were kept long enough to serve out their entire sentences.

Proper jails began to be built by individual counties in

This two-story log jail was built in the 1850s at Kerbyville (now Kerby).
(Josephine County Historical Society)

the late 1850s. By the middle of the next decade each jurisdiction had a place to keep—or try to keep—its outlaws.

Taking French Leave

Jailbreaks were not unusual in nineteenth-century Oregon. Probably half the men locked in jails managed to break out, or take "French leave," as the newspapers called it. A number of factors joined to produce the unearned freedom of many desperate characters who found themselves looking out between cold iron bars. Some jails were poorly constructed and badly maintained. Jail guards were sometimes unqualified, lazy, or crooked. Or they were incapacitated by their weakness for spirituous beverages. Often, particularly in small rural jails, the prisoners were

In 1858, the Polk County jail was built at Dallas, photo circa 1928. *(Polk County Historical Society)*

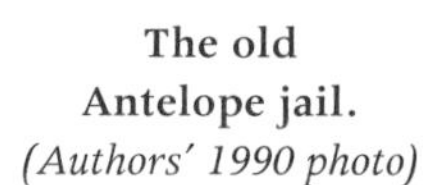

The old Antelope jail. *(Authors' 1990 photo)*

This vintage stone jail in Drewsey recalls the days in the 1880s when the wild town was called Gouge Eye. *(Authors' 1990 photo)*

The restored jail cells in the ghost town of Shaniko. *(Authors' photo)*

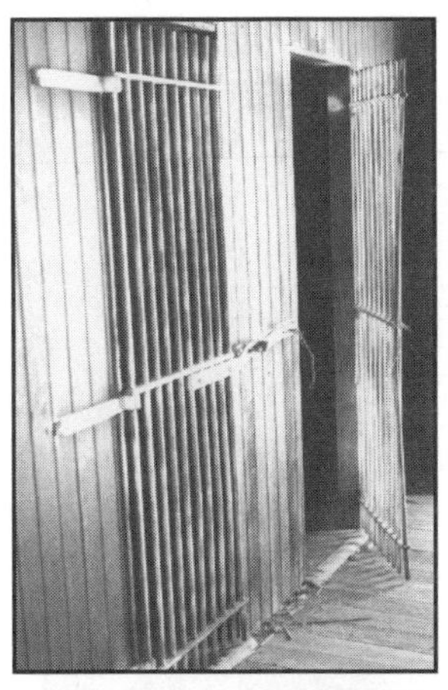

The single cell of the Antelope jail was stout enough to hold the worst outlaw. *(Authors' photo)*

The tiny Drewsey jail contained one cell. *(Authors' 1990 photo)*

In 1963, the old Greenhorn City jail was moved from its gold camp site to Canyon City, and now sits near the Grant County Museum. *(Authors' photo)*

left alone for long periods while the part-time jailer was elsewhere.

Few breaks involved violence, and some were humorous. One such story concerns the first jail built in Tillamook County in 1865, when the population of the entire county was less than 500. The jail building was built of round fir logs and was roofed with rudely fashioned shakes. As the first public building in the area, it was the pride of the local populous.

Shortly after the jail was completed, a man appeared at the office of the *Oregon Statesman* in Salem. He told editor Joseph Gaston that he had been falsely arrested, convicted, and jailed on a charge of hog thievery.

"I am not guilty!" he told the *Statesman*. "Bears ate those hogs, but I am not able to prove it. I am your only subscriber in Tillamook and I want you to get me a pardon from the governor."

Gaston notified the paper's owner, D.W. Craig, who decided that since paying subscribers were scarce in those parts, the best thing to do was to secure an interview for the visitor with Governor A.C. Gibbs. Together the innocent hog stealer and Mr. Craig called at the governor's office.

"But if you were convicted," asked the surprised governor, "what are you doing here in Salem?"

"I crawled up the inside logs, pushed the shakes aside and escaped from the roof," was the answer. "And now I'd like that pardon, please."

Governor Gibbs explained that he could not issue a pardon until he had seen a transcript of the trial and had proof that the fugitive actually was under sentence.

"There was no writing done at the trial," insisted the Tillamook man. "The justice of the peace just listened to the hog owner's story, and when I started to tell about the bears doin' it, he said I was guilty and put me in that new jail."

The astonished governor explained that while he could not grant an official pardon, he would give the Tillamook man a letter to take back suggesting to the justice of the peace that perhaps the accused had been jailed without due process of law.

"That's as good as a pardon," exclaimed the escapee triumphantly. "Nobody in Tillamook will know what 'due process of law' means."

In another case, the Crook County jail at Prineville was vacated one evening in 1892 when the sole occupant, a sheep thief named Alva Tupper, simply lifted up a floor board. The subsequent jail was not much better, for in another incident a prisoner left by removing part of the jail's wooden wall.

A Jacksonville man, George Justus, in the local jail for murder in 1884, broke out, leaving a note saying he had some urgent business to attend to and would return in a few days. He was found the next day at his mother's home.

Not all jailbreaks were comical. Though most early departures were accomplished on the sly, upon occasion a jailer was overpowered and sometimes hurt, or worse.

On July 4, 1888 two outlaws were sitting disconsolately in the Canyon City jail—a killer named Buckaroo Jim and Pat McGinnis, an accused horse thief. Buckaroo Jim later testified that on that day, Deputy Robert Lockwood laid his gun on a table when unlocking the cell. The shoeless McGinnis snuck up behind Lockwood, snatched the gun off the table, and shot the deputy twice, killing him. McGinnis was later caught, tried, and hanged.

Two desperadoes named Hall and Sproles, a murderer and a thief, broke out of the Union County jail in the spring of 1892. They had asked the jailer if they could wash their clothes and the kindly jailer agreed, unlocking their cell. The two began using a scrub board and tub in the corridor, but as soon as the trusting deputy turned his back, they jumped him and knocked him senseless. They then tied and gagged him, took the keys, and ran from the jail.

Fortunately, a blacksmith across the street saw what was happening, grabbed his rifle, and put a shot in front of the escapees. The men stopped, put up their hands, and were marched back to jail. No more clothes-washing for them.

Another fizzled jailbreak occurred in November 1898 at Eugene as Deputy Sheriff H.J. Day was bringing killer Claude Branton back to jail after a guilty verdict. The prisoner made a murderous assault on the deputy in an attempt to get his gun, but failed and was returned to his cell. However, in a few days he again made a bid for freedom. Branton had secretly fashioned a fake pistol out of a piece of wood and used it in an attempt to make Sheriff William Withers throw up his hands and let him out. The gun did not fool the sheriff, and the desperate killer remained in jail until his hanging.

Some jail escapes were carried out when the prisoners were left unguarded overnight. Take the classic jailbreak of Charlie Bassett. Bassett held up the stage near Grants Pass in early 1884 and after a lengthy manhunt was captured and put in the Jacksonville jail to await trial. In late August 1884, Charlie's fellow boarders in the jail were two murderers, George Justus and J.M. Culp, and embezzler James Watkins.

On the night of August 28, Charlie made his move. He knew the jailer did not sleep in the jail, opting instead for the more comfortable accommodations of a rented room up the street. Somehow, perhaps through a visitor, Charlie

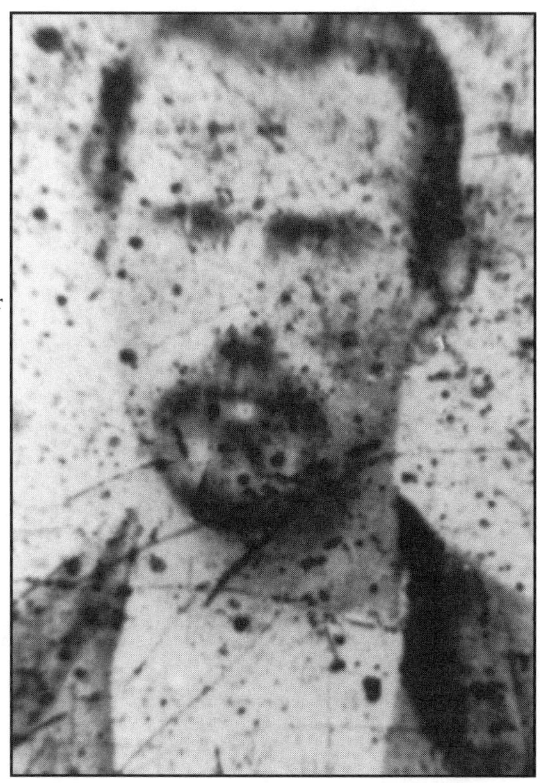

In the mid-1880s, stage robber Charlie Bassett found the Jacksonville jail not to his liking, so he left. *(Southern Oregon Historical Society)*

procured a small length of stiff wire and set about picking the lock on his cell door. After several hours of concentrated work, bending the wire into various shapes, the clever culprit finally succeeded in clicking open the lock.

Once out in the hallway, Bassett found himself faced with another obstacle, one more iron-barred door between him and freedom. In the outer room was a small, free-standing cabinet in which were kept the keys to the iron door and the various cell doors. But the cabinet was out of reach.

After some thought, the imaginative stage robber splintered a wooden dry goods box that was in the hallway. Using long narrow pieces from the box, and twisted strips of gunnysack material, Charlie fashioned a stick that, bound tightly with sacking, would bear its weight when held out. To the long stick he attached the stiff piece of wire, which he had bent into a hook. Next he carefully went fishing for the cabinet.

He finally succeeded in drawing the cabinet over to the iron door. With some further maneuvering, he was able to reach the keys and unlock the door. He then returned to the cells and let out his fellow roomers. They all went their own ways into the southern Oregon night.

The newspapers howled, the public yelled, and the sheriff, Abraham Jacobs, was red-faced and angry. He quickly gathered a posse to recapture the escapees. He did not have to look far for three of them. Watkins, the embezzler, gave himself up that same night. In fact, he went to the jailer's lodging room, woke him up, and told him about the jailbreak. Culp was captured the next day, as was George Justus. But there was no sign of Charlie Bassett, the clever mastermind of the breakout.

The jailbreak did not escape the notice of the newspapers. The Jacksonville *Democratic Times* said: "The jailer made a bad mistake in the jail that night." The *Oregon Sentinel* announced: "There has evidently been a want of vigilance on the part of the officials who have had these dangerous criminals in charge to have allowed them to escape." The *Ashland Tidings* pointed out the danger of Charlie's being on the loose: "Bassett, the stage robber who escaped from the county jail, had not been captured at last reports and is not likely to be. He will probably pay his respects to one of Wells Fargo's express box custodians somewhere in Oregon or California before many moons wax and wane."

Charlie Bassett was caught seven days later in the mountains, seventy miles from Jacksonville.

The Boys Get Stripes

The Oregon territorial fathers had a difficult time establishing a governmental penitentiary. In February 1851 the legislative assembly passed a bill for the construction of a prison in Portland that could house 100 inmates. The problem was that with all the political bickering and infighting over a location for the seat of government and other issues, the prison was not finished until 1857. The first murderer to enter the new brick-and-stone penitentiary was Cornelius Sharp, who had shot a man in an Oregon City bordello. The first female inmate, also Oregon's first murderess, was Charity Lamb, who had sunk an axe into her husband's head, later telling officials: "I didn't mean to kill the critter, I only meant to stun him."

When Cornelius, Charity, and sixteen others moved

Constructed of brick and stone in 1857, Oregon's first penitentiary was a long single-story building *(right center)* located on the south end of Front Street in Portland. *(Authors' collection)*

into their cells in Portland, it marked the beginning of the first regular prison in Oregon, the Territorial Penitentiary.

The high cost and inefficient management of the prison prompted the 1859 legislature of the brand-new state of Oregon to lease out the facility to private contractors. The lessees, Robert Newell and Levi English, subleased the prison to one Luzerne Besser. When Besser assumed control, there were twenty-five prisoners and shortly thereafter all twenty-five escaped. Most were recaptured. Luzerne Besser quit, and Newell and English defaulted to the state.

By the early 1860s there was considerable pressure to move the prison to the state capital at Salem. In 1865 land for a new penitentiary was selected within sight of the capitol building. In May 1866 the convicts were transported under heavy guard to their new home. Immediately, they began to escape. In the month of August 1866 there were 115 escapes from the new Salem penitentiary, including the massive breakout already related—fifty prisoners led by Matt Bledsoe.

This was also the era of the infamous Oregon Boot. The Oregon Boot, or Gardner Shackle, as it was known in those early days, was a restraining apparatus invented in 1865 by Portland prison warden J.C. Gardner. Patented by Gardner on July 3, 1866, the shackle was made in the prison blacksmith shop. The device consisted of a stirrup which fit under the bootsole of the convict and an attached thick iron band, weighing between fifteen and twenty-eight pounds, which was affixed and locked around the ankle.

With this weight on one leg and not on the other, a man found it impossible to run or walk very fast, and most found it difficult to get around at all. The early prison superintendents made liberal use of the Oregon Boot but the adverse effects on the health of the wearer, particularly

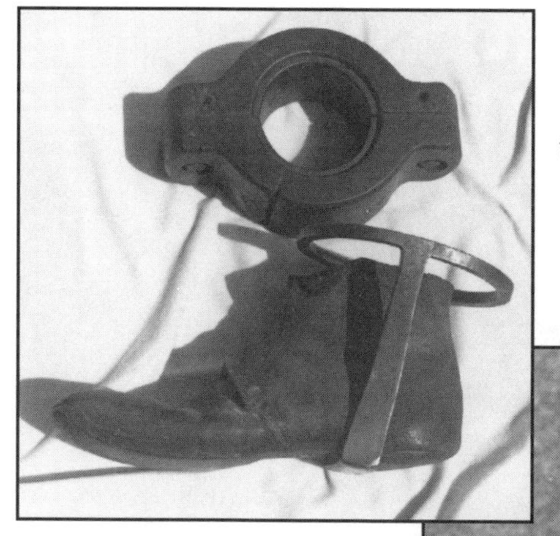

The infamous Oregon Boot was comprised of a stirrup that fit under the shoe and an attached ankle-band. *(Oregon State Sheriffs' Association)*

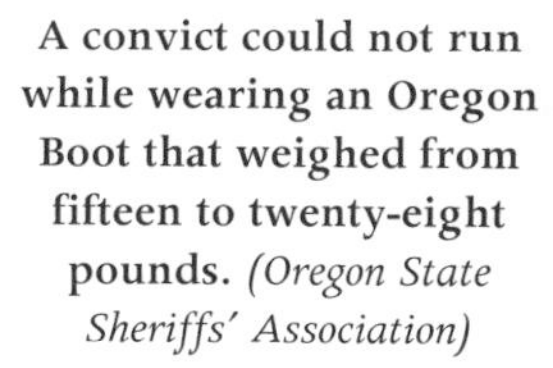

A convict could not run while wearing an Oregon Boot that weighed from fifteen to twenty-eight pounds. *(Oregon State Sheriffs' Association)*

upon the spine, caused the boot to be used only for specific punishment after 1878. After that time, by order of the governor, only convicts charged with attempted escape, fighting, or other serious breaches of the rules were "ironed down" in an Oregon Boot.

Thousands of Oregon Boots were made over the years. The device found widespread use throughout the United States and foreign countries. For although it was torture to the man wearing it, the Gardner Shackle did prevent escapes. The last manufacturer of the Oregon Boot was Art Burnside, who sold them in his police supply house in Spokane until the mid-1930s. Early-day Oregon Boots, now rare, command a price of up to $1,000 among collectors.

Much of the budget used to operate the Oregon State Penitentiary in the 1880s, 1890s, and early twentieth century came from industries within the walls. The

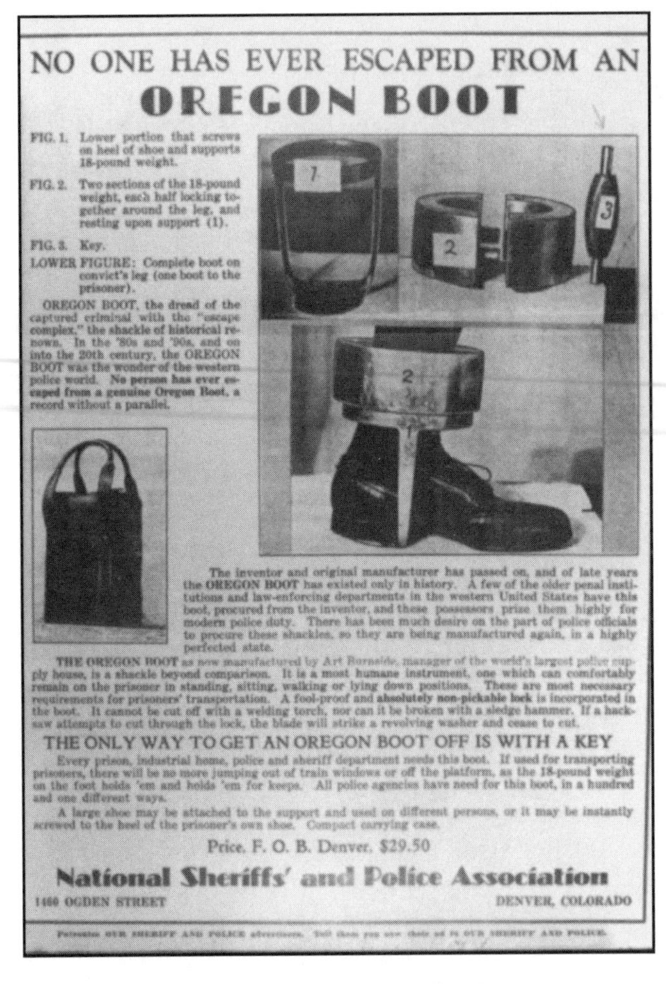

Advertisement for the Oregon Boot. *(Oregon State Sheriffs' Association)*

carpentry shop, blacksmith shop, tannery, flax mill, and shoemaking department turned out products for general sale as well as for use in the prison. There was even a soapmaking department for many years and a foundry where iron stoves were made.

By far the largest industry at the prison, and the one that caused the most difficulties because of escapes, was the brickyard. It was found that the land around the prison site contained clay that could be burned to produce quality bricks. Superintendent M.P. Berry established the brickyard during his administration from 1886 to 1870,

Oregon State Penitentiary in Salem, circa 1880s. *(Oregon State Archives)*

Warden James McKennon *(standing sixth from left)* and Oregon State Penitentiary staff in 1888. *(Oregon State Archives)*

and the manufacture of bricks became the prison's most dependable and profitable industry. In the summer of 1893, over 3,280,000 bricks were made for construction of state buildings and sale to private buyers. In 1915 brick manufacture tapered off, and by 1924 it had ceased entirely.

The brickyard was a favored place of employment for convicts planning an unauthorized vacation from the grounds, because it was located outside the prison walls. Old records show that second only to work parties far removed from the prison grounds, the brickyard was the point from which most escapees departed. In 1867 Flavius White got out of the brickyard twice, as did Jacob Kennedy in 1869. A new $176 brick burner was purchased in the

Old "A" Block in Oregon State Penitentiary, circa 1890. *(Oregon State Archives)*

summer of 1870 for the boys in the brickyard, but also in that year $1,405.50 was spent in chasing escaped prisoners, most having left from the same yard.

Even with the high number of escapes, making bricks was still the biggest industry at the penitentiary. Many state-owned and private buildings stand to this day in Oregon that were constructed with clay bricks from the old Salem pen brickyard.

Over the Wall with a Curse and a Prayer

Few events in old Oregon aroused public interest to a higher pitch than a well-publicized prison escape. County jail escapes were frequent enough to cause little comment outside the particular area affected, but an escape from Oregon's central stronghold was a different matter.

Certainly more than a few residents in districts where an escaped striper was seen were fearful of contact with him. In some cases, though, judging from the newspaper comments, there was a sort of sentimental sympathy for the underdog, and grudging admiration for the man with nerve enough to stake his life on a fling at the fortune wheel of liberty.

Most escapes from the penitentiary were made by convicts on work parties outside the walls. Occasionally, a prisoner who was kept inside had an overgrown bump of ingenuity and daring which prompted a carefully prepared scheme for going over the wall. Most of these plans, fortunately, did not include violence. Some required so much study, imagination, and planning that they would have done credit to an army general or a captain of finance.

Even if captured eventually, as they usually were, the escaped convicts who remained free for even a short while were generally accorded a certain amount of respect by

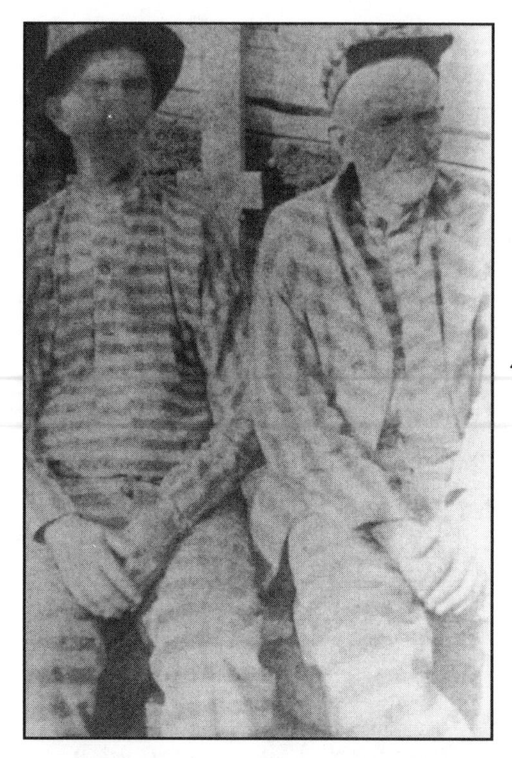

Oregon State Penitentiary "stripers," circa 1885. *(Oregon State Archives)*

Oregon "stripers" working outside the walls. *(Oregon State Archives)*

other inmates, and occasionally by the officials. However, that did not excuse the culprits from serving an extra period of time for their ill-advised capers.

Some of the escape attempts were bloody, dramatic affairs—the 1902 breakout of Tracy and Merrill, for example, and the earlier 1866 escape of Matt Bledsoe and the boys. There also was this incident:

In the summer of 1883 the state prison was enclosed by a wooden stockade. A massive brick wall was under construction but not yet finished. On July 3 of that year, Warden Collins and two other officers were seized by a group of desperate convicts in the prison brickyard. The men in stripes held their hostages at knife point and forced them to walk toward the main entrance in the wooden stockade.

The prisoner group swelled to fifty or sixty strong, and as they approached the gate, they demanded that the guard, Wilford Stillwell, open it or they would kill the warden. The guard opened the main gate and the convicts began rushing through. Warden Collins broke free, and Stillwell emptied his Sharp's rifle into the mass of stripes.

Many of the inmates fell back, and the warden managed to close the gate, but not until fourteen men had escaped. The guard quickly reloaded and brought down six of the fleeing convicts. The casualty list included three prisoners killed and four badly wounded. Warden Collins and Guard Stillwell were commended later that day by Governor Z.F. Moody for saving the penitentiary from complete disaster.

Doc and the Girls

In 1896, a humorous incident occurred at the Oregon State Penitentiary that was not intended as an escape—at least not at first. It involved a prisoner they called Doc, who worked in the prison hospital.

The female ward in those days was on the second floor of the administration building and was separated from the shoe shop by a brick wall about two feet thick. There was an old jailhouse saying that "love laughs at locks and bars." Brick walls could have been included, too. A year or two before, a section of the high wooden baseboard in the shoe shop had been neatly cut out, so that when loosely replaced it would not be noticed. A hole was then dug through the brick wall, leading into the storeroom of the women's ward.

By the underground system of communication found in all prisons, the six women inmates learned about the hole, and they set to work on their side of the wall. The women concealed the results of their labor by pasting newspapers around the room but attaching one over the hole so that it could be removed at will.

Two years later, Doc and a female accomplice were invited to the penitentiary for fifteen-year sentences for larceny. He began working in the prison hospital, and whenever the occasion permitted Doc patronized the secret hole in the wall. The companionship was enjoyed in a storeroom a short distance down the hall. It was dangerous business, but passion was strong between Doc and his lady.

One day Doc was tipped off that the matron would be away all afternoon, so he made for the hole at the first opportunity. Time flew by without notice, which the pair discovered to their sorrow. Just as they were about to leave, the matron's voice was heard in the hall. Accompanying her were one or two visitors, who held a lengthy conversation with the matron while standing in the corridor directly in front of the room with the secret hole. Doc could not escape to the hole, and the five o'clock bell was ringing. In five minutes, there would be a routine inmate count. But Doc was missing!

Doc had no choice but to remain missing. For nine days he stuck to that room, planning a way out. Food was slipped to him by the girls, usually biscuits, pieces of cold meat, and water. After the excitement died down, Doc prepared to make good his escape, intending to take his ladyfriend with him, dressed as a man in clothes smuggled through the hole. He planned to seize the matron, tie her up, and take her keys. He would then walk out with his accomplice.

One morning about five o'clock, he began to tie up the other women prisoners to save them from suspicious inquiry. His first victim was a game girl who was willing enough to be tied if it would help the romantic pair effect their escape. But the next girl, angling for a pardon, changed her mind about cooperating. She suddenly threw open a window and proceeded to wake most of western Oregon with her screeches. That settled it: Doc fled for the hole in the wall, intending to hide on the men's side. He was found within a few minutes, and the chagrined officials plugged the hole in the wall. And it stayed plugged. The tattle tale got her pardon.

The Tracy-Merrill Escape

> Run along, I've no time for a quitter;
> I have troubles enough to spare,
> And the prizes of life go to the man
> Who is ready to do and dare.
>
> old prison doggerel

At the Oregon State Penitentiary on the morning of June 9, 1902, Harry Tracy and David Merrill went over the wall with guns blazing and men dying. The desperadoes were front-page news across the country for many days, while determined bands of lawmen scoured the Pacific Northwest in a massive effort to run them to ground. It was one of the most famous and dramatic prison escapes ever to take place in the United States.

Harry Tracy, whose real name was Severns, was about twenty-seven years old when he arrived at the Salem prison in 1899. He was a killer, robber, and thief who had roamed through the Northwest for several years. By the time he reached Salem, he had already broken out of the Utah State Penitentiary and two jails in Colorado.

David Merrill, thirty years of age, arrived at Salem with Tracy. Merrill was an Oregon and Washington petty thief, lacking the steel nerve and audacity for anything more in the way of a criminal career. He had been in and out of jails since his teen years, including a couple of stretches in the Portland jail and a term in the Oregon State Penitentiary from January 31, 1890 to March 2, 1892 for larceny.

It is not known exactly when the two men became acquainted, but by the spring of 1898 they knew each other in Portland, where Tracy married Merrill's sister, Mollie, a dance hall girl. Tracy's mother-in-law, Amanda Merrill, known to the Portland police as Mother Merrill, was a gray-haired receiver of stolen goods.

In the fall of 1898 Harry Tracy and David Merrill teamed in a partnership of continuous crime, ranging from Portland to Seattle. By winter they had moved operations to their base city of Portland, where they engaged in a wave of robberies of saloons, stores, offices, and other small cash businesses. They wore costume masks and were soon dubbed by police as the "false face bandits."

Their profitable enterprise came to an end when Dave Merrill lost himself in the grip of old tanglefoot in a saloon

Harry Tracy was betrayed by his partner.
(Oregon State Archives)

David Merrill boasted of his exploits as one of Portland's "false face bandits."
(Oregon State Archives)

one night. He started bragging about how well they were doing, and a nearby customer overheard the boasts. Figuring Merrill for one of the well-publicized robbers, the eavesdropper told the police, and soon Detectives Dan Weiner and Joe Day were after Merrill.

The officers trailed the unsuspecting robber to his home, which they then raided and found a substantial amount of stolen jewelry, gold watches, and other items. Dave Merrill was arrested and, in a bid for leniency, set up his partner for a grab by the police. It was arranged for Harry to come to Merrill's house the next day, February 5, 1899. When he arrived, the police were waiting. After a running gunfight, during which Tracy was wounded, he was captured.

In a last bid for freedom, as Harry was being transported from his cell to the courtroom on March 21, he attempted to shoot his way out with a gun smuggled to him, probably by Mollie. After a short gun battle with Deputy Tom Jordan, the desperado gave up.

Tracy was sentenced to twenty years in prison, and Merrill was handed a thirteen-year term. They arrived at the front gate of the Salem pen on March 22, 1899. Soon, in striped convict's garb, they began work in the prison foundry.

From the moment the iron gate closed behind him, Tracy began planning his escape. On April 2, 1899 he wrote to his wife in Portland. On the front side of the paper Harry noted that he was well and made some suggestions to aid her welfare. But on the reverse side of the page, the cagey convict penned the real message. He wrote it in invisible ink, probably lemon juice, knowing that all mail was examined before leaving the prison. According to the *Oregon Journal,* word was sent by a friend for Mollie to hold the letter over a lamp to bring out its instructions to her.

The hidden letter, printed verbatim in the July 29, 1902 *Oregon Journal,* read as follows:

> Mollie. darling send me a ham and some sugar and coffee. cut the inside of the ham and put in a file and a saw and a brace in it. The saws are about the size of a corset steel. The brace wont cost much and will be handy to hold. Send them as soon as you can.
>
> Get a Colts with 25 cartridges. single action and get 25 cartridges for it. The brace is for saws. You can put everything in the ham. Send it to Robert E. Wilson. He has only a short time to serve.
>
> Answer right away and tell me if you get this. And you know where I told you to go if you hear about me getting away. Well goodbye darling little girl. I am nearly sure to break this time. Save your money so you dont get broke. Tracy

The appeal for breakout equipment went unheeded by Mollie Tracy, perhaps because she saw the folly of such an attempt. Harry would have to figure out something himself.

Time passed slowly for Tracy and Merrill. They caused constant trouble for the officials, leading to the duo being ironed down with dreaded Oregon Boots upon occasion. And they were closely watched.

Days turned to months, then to years without Harry Tracy developing a practical plan for going over the wall. But in early 1902, he came up with the idea for the Great Escape. It is probable that the first step of the plan was for Tracy to receive secret money from the outside to use as a bribe for an inside contact man. It was never determined who the inside helper was, either a convict or perhaps a guard, so let's call him Mr. X.

The plan next involved an inmate who was soon to be released. Some said it was a petty thief named Harry Wright, though another ex-con, Charlie Monte, was officially accused. Upon an alleged promise of $5,000, the outside man was to obtain two rifles and ammunition, which he would throw over the wall on a certain night. He first was to send a message to Mr. X inside the prison, telling him what night to expect the weapons to be put over the wall. Mr. X would retrieve the guns and hide them in a box in the foundry. There was to be an identifying chalk mark on the box.

As complicated and impractical as the plan sounds, it worked. Prison Superintendent Joseph D. Lee stated in an October 1902 report to the governor: "Their escape was accomplished by outside help. During the preceding night, probably, two rifles and a good supply of ammunition were secreted with the working tools of these two men."

That preceding night was June 8, 1902. The rifles,

Winchester .30-30s, came over the wall and into the box. The next morning Tracy and Merrill were ready.

On June 9, around 7 a.m., the usual line of about 150 prisoners began lock-stepping to the work shops, with Tracy and Merrill at or near the head of the line. When they entered their workroom, Tracy went immediately to the chalk-marked box and brought out a rifle. He took aim at the sole room guard, Frank S. Ferrall, who was standing with his back turned, and shot him twice in the head.

Merrill then snatched up the other rifle, and he and Tracy ordered the other prisoners to the opposite side of the workroom. The two armed convicts next ran to a window facing the yard and began firing at the guards on the wall. After shooting several shots, Tracy and Merrill ran through a passage into adjoining shops. Here they encountered a life convict named Fred Ingram, who attempted to wrest the rifle away from Dave Merrill. Breaking free of Ingram's grasp, Merrill shot him in the left knee. (Ingram's leg was later amputated, but he won a pardon for his courageous efforts.)

Convict Fred Ingram was shot while trying to prevent the Tracy-Merrill escape, but he earned a pardon for his heroic effort. *(Oregon State Archives)*

After this shooting, they made their way through the carpenter's shop, pausing to pick up a wooden ladder used for oiling machinery. Then Tracy and Merrill ran out toward the west wall. When they emerged from the building, they were shielded by piles of old boxes. They began firing at the guards in the southwest and northwest towers. None was hit, though one of the bullets did pass through the hat of a guard named Ross.

By this time the entire prison was in an uproar, with frantic guards trying to control the excited prison population and at the same time attempting to bring down the two armed men. A fusillade of shots spewed down on Tracy and Merrill, who returned a steady fire as they worked their way along the side of the building. Reaching the end of the shop buildings, the outlaws turned around the corner to the north wall, firing as they ran across the open space. Tracy drew a quick bead on the tower guard, S.R. Jones, who was exposed, and killed him with a well-placed shot.

In a hail of bullets, the fleeing prisoners leaned the ladder against the wall and climbed over, dropping to the ground outside. They ran east along the wall until, turning the northeast corner, they came face to face with guards Ross and Tiffany. Catching the guards by surprise, the escapees ordered them to put up their hands and march ahead.

Merrill picked up the guards' guns and took their ammunition. Using the hostages as shields, the convicts reached a position of safety out of the wall guards' sight. They ordered the captive guards to go back, but as they ran toward the prison, Tracy calmly shot Tiffany in the back, killing him. At the sound of the shot, Ross threw himself to the ground and was not hit.

The two killers quickly scrambled south into the

nearby woods, where they disappeared. Superintendent Lee immediately notified Marion County Sheriff Frank W. Durbin and Salem City Marshal Gibson. Within the hour, a large, heavily armed posse formed outside the walls and the search began.

Although the roads and bridges south of Salem were guarded, and the surrounding countryside swarming with searchers, nothing was seen of the escaped convicts by lawmen that night. But at least three people not associated with the posses did see them. At about ten o'clock the two killers left the copse of woods south of Salem, where they had been hiding, and returned warily to town. There they held up J.W. Roberts and Roy Ohmart, stole the men's clothes, and abandoned their stripes in a pile behind some bushes. Then they broke into Felix Labranche's stable and took two horses.

The next day, June 10, was a busy one for the lawmen. Two bloodhounds were rushed by train from the Walla Walla penitentiary, arriving in Salem by noon. About that time, Sheriff Durbin was notified that Tracy and Merrill had forced their way into the cabin of a woodcutter named August King, near the village of Gervais, and demanded some food. Upon departing, the escapees had left the stolen horses at the cabin and were last seen running into the woods about one mile east of Gervais. Durbin brought the dogs and a large party of men to the scene by train.

All through the day the manhunters scoured the area for Tracy and Merrill. The bloodhounds picked up their scent at the King cabin and led the lawmen through fields, forests, and thick brush. Circling, dodging, backtracking, and circling again, the fugitives stayed ahead and out of sight of their pursuers. Then the dogs lost the trail.

At dusk, two searchers in a buggy, Dr. C.S. White and Edward DuPuis, were stopped at gunpoint along the road

Bloodhounds and lawmen on the trail of Tracy and Merrill in Salem. *(Oregon State Archives)*

to Gervais by the fleeing felons. The killers took the men's weapons and clothing, and, with a comment about needing them worse than the doctor, they also took the horse and buggy.

Like characters in a dime novel, the outlaws taunted the authorities with their daring. Late that night they suddenly appeared in Gervais at the house of Mr. L. Briggs, where they stole food and clothes. That same night they were seen in a livery stable in town and it was surmised that they slept in some hidden corner of Gervais.

About four o'clock the next morning, June 11, the boys made an even more surprising move: they worked their way east of town again, right into the primary area of the manhunt, and once more called on their unwilling host of the previous morning, August King. After taking breakfast with the terror-stricken woodcutter, the fugitives struck for the nearby woods. The Walla Walla bloodhounds again picked up the scent and went baying off into the countryside, followed by determined lawmen, but the difficult chase through brush and woods was to no avail.

In the early afternoon, Company "D" of the Oregon National Guard arrived from Woodburn to assist the civilian authorities. The intensive search continued, but there was no trace of the elusive, dangerous quarry. Now over 200 men were in the area looking for Tracy and Merrill.

Finally, late that day, one of the possemen spotted the fugitives in a wheat field adjoining a thick woods near a crossroads about two miles east of Gervais. Immediately the word went out. Within hours the entire force of searchers converged on the spot of the sighting. The area, near what is now the crossing of Howell Prairie Road and Mt. Angel-Gervais Road, comprised patchwork farms set amidst heavy stands of timber and thickets of dense brush.

Sheriff Durbin and the other posse leaders deployed men all the way around the periphery of the island of trees

The field and woods near Gervais where Tracy and Merrill were surrounded.
(Authors' photo)

and heavy vegetation Tracy and Merrill had run into. Some men were sent in with dogs, but they were fired upon from an unseen vantage point deep within the thicket.

As nightfall approached, the decision was made to protect the men and dogs by waiting until daylight for further searching. The plan was to keep the fugitives penned inside the woods through the night. About 250 men were stationed at close intervals around the grove, and bonfires ringed the trees in an effort to prevent undetected escape. Sheriff Durbin announced to the press that capture was imminent.

But something went wrong. Many members of the immense posse said it was too dark to distinguish one another from the civilian-attired convicts. Others said it was because certain possemen left their posts to mingle and visit with friends elsewhere on the line. Still others were accused of sleeping at their positions, and some were said to have tired of the game and gone home. Whatever the reasons, the fact was that upon a massive surge through the woods the next morning, the lawmen found that Tracy and Merrill were not there. They had escaped during the night, leaving the ring of men to guard squirrels and rabbits and a few deer.

Just after seven o'clock that same morning, June 12, Tracy and Merrill were seen near the settlement of Monitor, six miles east of the grove from which they escaped. At Monitor they forced their way into the house of A. Akers, where only two women were present. "I am Tracy," came the announcement, followed by a demand for food.

The next sighting came later that day at Needy, six miles northeast of Monitor, when the fugitives called at the home of Edward Graves. Again, the pronouncement "I am Tracy" brought terrified cooperation from the Graves household.

That was the last time Tracy and Merrill were positively identified in Oregon until the morning of June 15, when they forced two farmers, George Sunderland and Walter Burlingame, to ferry them across the Columbia River, landing five miles above Vancouver, Washington. There they held up one farmer and took the clothes from a second, whom they bound and gagged, and then fled into the timber.

From then on, this most remarkable chase led through many parts of Washington. Fears turned to panic and many people were afraid to leave their homes. Strangers were scrutinized and avoided, barking dogs were heeded, and everywhere people waited for those terror-striking words: "I am Tracy."

On June 28, Tracy killed Dave Merrill near Napavine, north of Castle, Washington, in retribution for Merrill's having turned him in. On August 5, exhausted from the chase, Harry Tracy sought refuge at the Eddy Ranch, southeast of Creston, Washington. There, after a lengthy running gunfight with lawmen during which he was wounded twice, the trapped killer finally ended the long hunt by shooting himself in a cornfield.

The end of Harry Tracy. *(Oregon State Archives)*

CHAPTER 9

HIGH SCAFFOLDS AND HEMP

Men are not hanged for stealing horses,
but that horses may not be stolen.
Marquis of Halifax
17th-century essayist

WHAT WAS IT ABOUT HANGINGS that drew such crowds? People came from farms and settlements for miles around, to the place where an unhappy miscreant was to be strung up. When George Beale and George Baker were hanged for murdering Salem's Daniel Delaney in 1865, a crowd of at least 1,000 spectators thronged the public square. Little girls were seen carrying picnic lunches, and it was a gala affair for all but the two Georges and the sheriff who dropped them. When William Kendall was hanged in '51 for killing William Hamilton, a public holiday was proclaimed. When Berry Wey met the rope at Canyon City in 1863, the mines shut down for the occasion, the school was let out, and a circus atmosphere pervaded the town.

Indeed, the pioneers found few events more entertaining than a public hanging. In 1859, even Salem's statehood celebration was outshone by the hanging of Charlie Roe. Achieving statehood caused only mild public

The grisly Dallas hanging of William Lardith on July 6, 1890 was shielded from the curious crowd by a high fence. *(Polk County Historical Society)*

excitement because it was anticlimactic after the long process of getting there. Charlie's hanging, however, brought hundreds of people, including over 200 women and children, thronging to the gallows. Charlie had murdered his wife because he suspected infidelity. He had loved her, he told the sheriff, but killed her to prevent others from enjoying her. So on April 2, 1859, Charlie Roe became the first man executed in the brand-new state of Oregon.

Oregon's early sheriffs had the unpleasant task of executing convicted killers, and hanging was the only legal means. Most sheriffs were reluctant to hang a man, though it was their sworn duty to do so. Thus, in 1887, when saloonkeeper Chris Caldwell killed Charles Kean in the rowdy Siskiyou railroad construction camp called Helltown, the resultant jury verdict was just fine with the sheriff.

Chris and Charlie fought over a girl and Chris lost. He went back to his saloon, armed himself with a revolver, without a word grabbed Kean around the neck, pressed the gun against him, and promptly ended Charlie's worldly troubles.

It was a sure bet for first-degree murder—and a hanging. When the jury brought back a verdict of only second-degree, most Helltown residents were highly displeased. It meant, though, the sheriff did not have to go through the ordeal of hanging a man.

On the occasions when an execution had to be carried out, temporary scaffolds were erected in jail yards. By the 1890s, high board fences were built around the gallows to ensure that the ceremony was private and dignified. Only invited witnesses, the necessary officials, and the condemned man were permitted behind the enclosure.

Execution of killer John Gilman at Empire on May 12, 1889.
(Coos County Museum Collection)

Claude Branton stands on the trapdoor in the Eugene jail yard on May 12, 1898. Sheriff William Withers is on far right. *(Oregon State Sheriffs' Association)*

Because many invitations were usually issued, the crowds inside were large, and the throngs outside larger still.

In 1900, when W.G. Magers was to hang for killing Raymond Sink, Polk County Sheriff J.G. Van Orsdel constructed a 40′ x 40′ board enclosure on the courthouse square in Dallas. On February 2, the day of the execution, about 100 spectators, bearing printed invitations, were allowed inside the high board fence. About 500 others stood outside, unable to see the proceedings, but eager to participate in the carnival atmosphere. Even a drenching rain did not deter them.

Hangings took place from the earliest years of Oregon's history until 1914, when Governor Oswald West led a drive to abolish capital punishment in the state. The measure squeaked by with only a 157-vote majority. In 1920 capital punishment was reestablished, and later the method of

The Dalles, Oregon, July 13th 1905

Mr. Martin White

You are hereby invited to be present and witness the execution of NORMAN WILLIAMS on

Friday, July 21st, 1905,

at the hour of 6 o'clock, a. m., within the enclosure of the Wasco County Jail Yard in The Dalles, Oregon.

R C Sexton

Sheriff of Wasco County, State of Oregon.

NOT TRANSFERABLE. Present this card for admittance.

☞Norman Williams was convicted of the crime of murder in the first degree for the killing of one, Alma Nesbit, at Hood River, Oregon. Convicted May 28, 1904. Re-sentenced, after appeal, June 10, 1905.

The admission of witnesses inside the scaffold fence was by invitation only. On July 13, 1905, Norman Williams became the last man to be publicly hanged in the county of the crime. All subsequent executions took place at the Oregon State Penitentiary. *(Oregon State Sheriffs' Association)*

execution was changed to lethal gas. The last public hanging took place at The Dalles in 1905, when Norman Williams dropped through the trap for a double murder. After the Williams case, all hangings took place at the state penitentiary in Salem.

Here are a few cases that led the outlaws up thirteen steps to a platform, a group of solemn witnesses, and a waiting noose.

Berry Wey

In the early 1860s the boisterous, wide-open gold camp of Canyon City tolerated rowdy conduct and even gunfights. One-sided, cold-blooded murder, however, was another matter.

John Gallagher ran a successful pack train operation in 1863 from Canyon City to The Dalles, and the trustworthy packer often carried gold out to The Dalles for shipment to San Francisco. In that year he took on a partner named Berry Wey, a stranger at Canyon City, who, like other desperate characters, had come to the boomtown seeking to strike it rich without grubbing in the hills.

The two men started out from Canyon City for The Dalles with a string of horses and thousands of dollars in gold. In the free and easy way of those days, when partnerships were casual and changed often, no one thought much about it when Berry Wey showed up alone at The Dalles. He said his partner, Gallagher, had sold the operation to him and left the country. But when Wey was seen with Gallagher's unique revolver with "J.G." cut in the white bone grips, suspicions were aroused.

Soon miners on their way to Canyon City found the body of John Gallagher on Cherry Creek, near present Mitchell, where it had been dug up by coyotes. He had been shot.

Meanwhile, Berry Wey hightailed it to Idaho Territory. Deputy Sheriff Frank McDaniel, who headquartered in Canyon City, was sent to find him, and he captured his quarry around the Oro Fino mines of Idaho and brought him back for trial.

In remote sections of eastern Oregon, resorting to regular courts for adjudication of cases was infrequent unless the crime occurred conveniently near a seat of government. Since Grant County, of which Canyon City would become the county seat in 1864, had not yet been established, the court was far away at The Dalles. Therefore, trials conducted in Canyon City were by the "miners' meeting" method that came into favor during the California gold rush of '49. At a miners' meeting a large group of miners sat as a quasi-legal tribunal to hear and rule on cases. A chairman was elected and the entire assemblage of miners acted as a jury. Miners' meeting verdicts were not vigilante actions. They were surprisingly fair to the defendants on trial, though many did result in hangings. And a panel of miners was certainly closer to "a jury of his peers" than a defendant would face in a regular court.

In any event, the miners' meeting style of popular justice was in effect at Canyon City in 1863 when a somber Berry Wey was brought to trial. The miners gathered, leaders were chosen for roles as judge, prosecutor, and defense attorney, and the matter was tried.

Berry was convicted of murdering John Gallagher and sentenced to hang. It was Canyon City's first hanging and they wanted to do it right. A gallows was built on the summit of the hill near the cemetery. At the miners' expense, Berry was provided a new suit of clothes in which to be hanged. When the time came, two days after the trial,

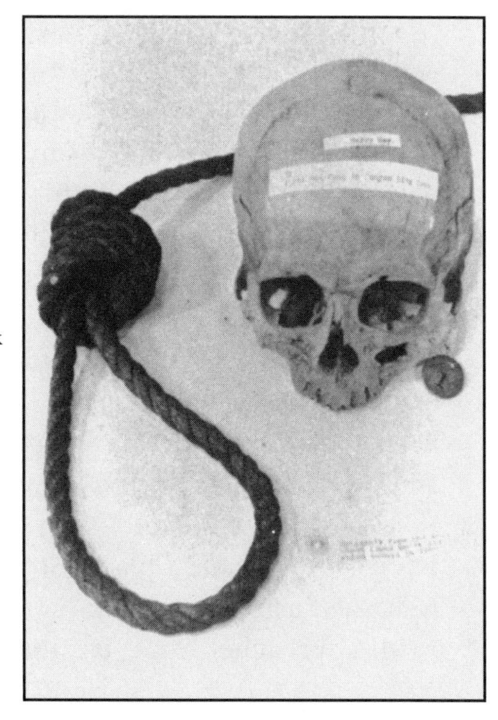

Berry Wey's skull and the noose that hanged him are on display at the Grant County Museum as stark reminders of justice in the early mining days of Canyon City. *(Grant County Museum Collection)*

he was taken up the hill in a wagon. On the ride to his rope he sat on the pine box that was to be his coffin. It is said that he yelled out to followers, "Don't run boys, nothing will happen 'til I get there." When all was ready, Frank McDaniel sprung the trap and Canyon City had its first hanging.

The Hanging of Two Georges

In Salem the year 1865 was ushered in on a cold, windy rainstorm. What dampened the spirits of the local residents was not the rain, they were used to that. What saddened and shocked them was the murder of a kind, generous farmer named Daniel Delaney. The elderly man usually called Uncle Daniel was an Oregon pioneer who had crossed the plains in '43 with such notables as Jesse Applegate and Dr. Marcus Whitman. Delaney's good-natured helpfulness was renowned in the area.

Uncle Daniel had been in the habit of keeping overnight guests, and one of these was George F. Beale, an itinerant butcher. Beale had noticed a wooden keg under Delaney's bed. Since the prosperous farmer was said to have gold hidden somewhere on his place—there was no bank in the district at the time—Beale figured the keg contained the golden hoard. And he wanted it.

The butcher's dark intentions solidified when he heard Uncle Daniel had just made a large and profitable cash sale of cattle. Beale confided his knowledge of the gold-laden keg to a saloonkeeper of low reputation, one George Baker, and together the men made a plan.

At dusk on January 9, Beale and Baker rode out toward the Delaney place. Stopping at a watering trough near the farm, the two blackened their faces as a disguise, then approached the farmhouse. The details of what happened next were later related by the one eyewitness to the terrible affair. Beale and Baker assumed Daniel Delaney was home alone, not realizing a young boy named Jack DeWolf was also present.

George Beale walked up to the front door and knocked, while Baker stood at the gate. When Delaney came to the door, Beale asked directions to the house of Daniel, Jr., Delaney's son. It was not clear if Uncle Daniel immediately recognized Beale, but he came out of the house and into the yard to point the way. As he did so, George Baker, still near the front gate, shot him. Delaney was knocked to the ground by the shot but staggered to his feet. The boy, remaining in the house, heard Uncle Daniel exclaim: "I know you, Beale, for God's sake don't kill me. I'll give you all the money I've got." Beale answered, "Old man, dead men tell no tales." He then shot Uncle Daniel between the eyes.

Young Jack DeWolf quickly locked the front door. When the two men began breaking it down, he escaped out the back and hid in a woodpile. After shivering in his hiding place all night, the lad ran to the home of Uncle Daniel's son at first light to report the tragedy.

Marion County Sheriff Sam Headrick was soon on the case, and it was not long before he had the killers in chains. Trial was held in Judge Reuben P. Boise's court. The two Georges, Beale and Baker, were convicted and sentenced to hang. They later confessed to the murder and said they found only $1,400 in the house. They said they buried the money by a stream, though it was never recovered. Where exactly they found the money in the house remains a mystery, too. It certainly was not in the wooden keg, for it turned out that Uncle Daniel kept only his supply of nails in it!

The double hanging was set for May 17, 1865 at the

public square in Salem. A scaffold was constructed in a small grove of oaks at present South Church and Bellevue Streets, near the north approach to the Pringle Creek bridge. The two killers went to their ropes in bad humor, kicking and fighting. One tried to spit on one of Uncle Daniel's sons as the noose was adjusted. When all was ready, Sheriff Headrick prayed, then dropped the two Georges to their dark rewards.

There were 1,000 spectators at the open ceremony, including school children carrying their lunches.

The End of William Cain

During the winter of 1865, a Canyon City miner named William Cain worked for months without pay, but with a promise of payment in the spring. His employer, a well-liked mine owner named Andy Watson, was true to his word, in a manner of speaking. When springtime came to the Canyon City mines Watson did pay off Bill Cain, but in greenbacks, not gold. Greenbacks were national bank notes issued by the United States Treasury to help boost a flagging economy due to the turmoil following the Civil War. They were backed by U.S. bonds instead of gold. (Greenbacks would not be convertible into gold until 1879.)

Greenbacks were highly unpopular with frontier workingmen. To them money meant gold, not pieces of paper. And greenbacks were totally unacceptable to Cain. He had spent many years toiling in the mines, and, through bad luck and bad judgment, had not been able to scrape together any significant amount of money. To Bill Cain, the $100 due him for working through a bitter eastern Oregon winter represented a substantial stake. After waiting patiently for payday to arrive with the spring, he wasn't going to put up with the despised greenbacks.

When Cain's several ardent requests to be paid in real money—gold—were rebuffed, he lost control. He went to his tiny cabin, got his pistol, and shot his former employer to death. There were witnesses to the shooting. When Watson's body was pulled from the Canyon Creek flume, Cain was charged with murder.

At that time there was a colorful character named Cincinnatus Hiner Miller, more popularly known as Joaquin Miller, a newspaperman, prospector, and adventurer, who would later gain national recognition as the Poet of the Sierra. In June 1865, at Canyon City, Oregon, the county seat of brand-new Grant County, Miller was working as a lawyer. And he had a very unpopular client in one William Cain.

Cincinnatus Hiner Miller— "Joaquin Miller"— was a Canyon City attorney. *(Authors' collection)*

After Andy Watson had been murdered, talk ran high against the accused greenback-hating miner, and it was all Sheriff M.P. Berry could do to keep him safe for the jury. As Joaquin Miller set about preparing Cain's defense, he himself was the target of verbal slights and disapproval by some of the deceased's many friends.

Then came the trial. Lawyer Miller waxed eloquent in pleading his client's case. The matter was not one of cold-blooded murder, he said, but an unfortunate, tragic case of irresistible impulse. It had been brought about by the deceased's total lack of regard for the defendant's impassioned pleas to be paid in real and proper money for the strenuous, productive work performed by the loyal, uncomplaining, hardworking defendant. It was not, surely, a case of murder but a circumstance of passion, a matter of a simple man wishing to be honorably and rightly paid for the only thing of value he possessed, his bodily labor. It was a case of *quid pro quo*—something for something.

William Cain was quickly found guilty of murder and sentenced to hang.

In Joaquin Miller's file on the case he noted: "The rulings of the Court in this case were severe throughout. Defendant was found guilty and sentenced to die. Executed on Aug 3rd 1865. Died as he lived!"

The Church Street Murderer

Poor old Lewis McDaniel. If the Fates bestow a man of age with a young, comely wife, they should at least have the decency to compel her to be satisfied with her lot. But in the case of Amanda McDaniel, his alluring spouse, that was not to be. And tragedy resulted.

At about 7:30 p.m. on November 20, 1884, in the Siskiyou foothills community of Ashland, a passerby walking along Church Street stumbled upon a man lying in the road. It was kindly Lewis McDaniel, a neighborhood resident. He had been shot at close range with a shotgun.

The murder of McDaniel was puzzling. He was found fifty yards from his front gate and had a sum of money in his pocket. McDaniel had no enemies, he was not involved in any nefarious activities, and he was respected in Ashland, where apparently he lived quietly with his wife.

Though a number of people in the area heard a shotgun blast, no one looked out at the time because a gunshot was not unusual in those days—perhaps someone shooting a varmint, or maybe a drunk firing at the moon. But pretty Amanda was now a widow.

During the subsequent investigation by Jackson County Sheriff Abraham Jacobs, it was learned that the most likely candidate as a suspect in the terrible slaying was a local n'er-do-well named Lewis O'Neil. As people came forward with information, a somewhat different picture of the quiet McDaniel household began to emerge.

It seems that Lewis O'Neil, a big, dark-haired, dark-eyed, handsome fellow, quite married, had been dallying with Mrs. McDaniel of late. In fact, the gossips said, certain things were seen going on between O'Neil and Amanda right there in the McDaniel house while the husband was away. Indeed, some claimed McDaniel had recently had hot words with O'Neil, and had warned him to keep away from his house and his wife. For several nights before the murder O'Neil had been seen lurking about the neighborhood after dark.

Within a couple of days the figurative noose had tightened around O'Neil. His boots matched tracks left in the soft mud at the murder site, and a shotgun was found hidden nearby, an old-style barrel-loading type. A charge of buckshot was still in one of the barrels wadded with newspaper. A paper with that exact piece torn out was found at O'Neil's house. Finally, the shotgun was identified by an unusual stock carving as one owned by George O'Neil, Lewis' older brother. George had sold the gun to Lewis sometime before the killing.

Lewis O'Neil was arrested, indicted for murder, and held in the jail at Jacksonville pending a trial. On March 12, 1885, he was found guilty and sentenced to hang by Judge Lionel Webster. The fateful day was set for May 21, but the date was postponed when O'Neil appealed his case to the Oregon Supreme Court. When the court denied his appeal, a new execution date was set for March 12, 1886.

Those were the facts in the Church Street Murder case, but what made it unusual was what Lewis O'Neil did while sitting in jail awaiting his date with the rope. Lewis knew he had little chance of escaping the gallows on his own, so he came up with the grand idea of having someone else confess to the McDaniel murder. If he had been killed by another, of course, Lewis O'Neil could not have done it. A good plan, but there was one small detail to accomplish: getting someone to confess to a murder they had not committed.

He first tried his erstwhile paramour, the lovely widow McDaniel. O'Neil wrote her a letter, evidently hoping she still favored him. Her ardor had likely paled, though, because before his trial, Lewis had suggested that Amanda had actually planned the murder—he had just carried it out for her. The Widow McDaniel was charged as an accomplice, based on Lewis' assertions, but had been found not guilty at her trial.

Now he was writing to her with this simple request: "It is in your power to save my life. You can do it by coming to town and swear that you did the killing and that I had neither hand, act, or part of it or any knowledge of it."

He then went on to explain that she could not be tried again for the same crime, and that if he were set free by her aid, he would sue the State of Oregon and divide equally with her. There is no record that Amanda ever responded to this tempting offer by the man who had gotten her into trouble in the first place.

Lewis O'Neil then penned another letter, this time to a friend, a Mr. Johns. In it he wrote: "Try to get someone to clear me by swearing they done the killing...Then they can clear themselves by proving where they were on the 20th of Nov. 1884, the night McDaniel was killed." Again Lewis offered to sue the authorities and split with his benefactor. Difficult as it may be to understand, however, Johns refused to come forward to perjure himself with a false confession of murder.

Now Lewis was getting desperate. His friends had abandoned him and the noose was just days away. Why not turn to family? Thus, on March 3, 1886, he wrote his most shameful request of all in a letter to his older brother, George, who was seventy-four. It was a long, rambling diatribe against the authorities, the law, and his unjust predicament. He complained of ill health, not being able to see the sun, and the disgrace of leaving his six children to the "mercy of the world without protection."

Then he made his plea: "As for you, you have lived to be a very old man and in the natural course of events you can expect to live but a few years more and are liable to drop off at any time. If you had but one hour to live it would be a hard request to ask you to come and state that you done the killing and that I was not any hand, act, or part of it or any knowledge of it. That would clear me and spare me to my children and only on their account I could never think of making such a request of you. This is the only thing that can save me."

Lewis went on to suggest that brother George's confession should be in writing, be witnessed by three people, and be made in the county clerk's office. He cautioned George to come right away as "the time being short, there is not a moment to fool away." Then he closed the letter: "Hoping to hear from you, I remain your loving brother. Lewis O'Neil."

Brother George did not answer.

On March 12, 1886, on a scaffold built in the narrow space between the Jackson County courthouse and the jail, before a sizable audience, Lewis O'Neil, the Church Street killer, dropped through the trap.

He had run out of ideas.

Jackson County Sheriff Abraham Jacobs *(right)* and Father F.X. Blanchet *(left)* stand on the scaffold with murderer Lewis O'Neil *(center)* before his hanging on March 12, 1886 in Jacksonville. *(Oregon State Sheriffs' Association)*

CHAPTER 10

Badges in the Dust

The tales of Oregon's outlaws are also the stories of the lawmen who pursued them. A number of courageous officers have been met in these pages, and there were many others. Tough, tenacious Douglas County Sheriff Frank Hogan, for instance, who often chased his prey hundreds of miles. Little-known lawmen such as Ezra Eby, who kept the peace in early Redmond with a .45 and a star cut from the back of an old watch case. Portland's famous 1890s detective Joe Day, who followed the worst of criminals into the very heart of their North End and waterfront dens, armed with only a tiny nickel-plated pistol and sharp wits. M.G. Sullivan of Thiel's Detective Service, whose sole purpose in life was to catch bank robbers in the 1880s and 1890s.

Lawmen faced difficult and perilous tasks in carrying out their work in old Oregon, with poor or no roads, great distances to be traveled on horseback, and lack of easy communication. Men who toted a badge in those days often worked alone, trailing and facing their quarry without help, learning by necessity to be alert and resourceful. Through dogged determination and tireless tracking—

without the aid of computers or laboratories—the early lawmen in general provided excellent service to the Oregon public, from the cobbled streets of Portland to the vast sage plains east of the Cascades. And they usually got their man.

Unfortunately, some of those brave law officers became victims of the outlaws they were pursuing. Here are the stories of four dedicated men who sacrificed themselves for their duty.

Sheriff William W. Withers, Lane County

It was dark by the time Sheriff Bill Withers and his two deputies approached the tiny settlement of Walton in the Coast Range. Snow draped western Lane County in silence, and the men and horses were tired after the nearly thirty-mile ride from Eugene. The date was February 5, 1903, and they were hunting a man.

Edward Elliott Lyons was a thirty-five-year-old horse thief and petty criminal who had most recently operated in the Rogue River country of southern Oregon, though he had previously lived in Lane County. His criminal record included a year spent in prison for embezzlement: He had been hired as a deputy sheriff to collect taxes, but had pocketed the money. Upon his release, Lyons drifted down to Jackson County, where he committed a number of thefts.

Next he stole some horses near Medford. He was caught and jailed in Jackson County, but soon escaped through a ruse pulled on the jailer. He promptly headed north to Lane County, where his wife and parents lived in a house near Walton.

Bill Withers was a likable, gregarious man who was enjoying his reputation as one of the friendliest yet most efficient sheriffs Lane County had ever seen. He was a family man, handsome, fair in all dealings, and competent.

Murderer Elliott Lyons. *(Oregon State Sheriffs' Association)*

Lane County Sheriff William W. Withers. *(Oregon State Sheriffs' Association)*

The people of the county were looking forward to his continued term of office and the possibility that he would afterward seek even higher positions of public service.

On February 3, Bill had learned from someone living in the west county district around Walton that Elliott Lyons had been seen at his family's house. The sheriff obtained an arrest warrant on the Jackson County horse-stealing charge and on the morning of February 5 started to Walton to bring Lyons in. As a precautionary measure, Withers took with him Constable Jack Smith of Eugene.

After a long, cold horseback ride, with rest stops at Elmira and Hale's Stage House near present Noti, Withers and Smith picked up a third man to assist them, a Walton area homesteader named Will Cornelius, whom the sheriff deputized. The three men reached the Lyons house at seven o'clock that evening.

Their plan was to make a quiet approach to the house on foot, leaving the horses some distance away. Smith and Cornelius would go to the back to prevent an escape that way. When they were properly positioned, Smith would whistle, and the sheriff would knock on the front door to confront the fugitive.

It was learned later that after hearing Jack Smith's whistle, Sheriff Withers knocked on the front door. After a few moments, during which the sounds of scurrying about could be heard from within the house, the front door was opened by Lyons' wife. The sheriff apologized for his unannounced visit, showed her the warrant, and explained that he had come for Elliott. Mrs. Lyons backed into the room and Withers, his revolver still in its holster, followed.

Lyons' father and mother were in the kitchen, and the sheriff again expressed his regret that the visit was for such an unhappy purpose. Elliott Lyons then made his appearance from another room. At that point the two women, wailing and screaming for the lawman not to take Lyons away, suddenly rushed at him. They pinioned Withers' arms to his sides, beseeching him to leave Elliott alone. He struggled to throw the women off, and he told Lyons he was under arrest for horse-stealing and escape. Lyons drew a .38 revolver from his belt and shot the sheriff in the neck.

Bill Withers fell to the floor. Elliott Lyons bolted out the front door and ran into the night. Smith and Cornelius came into the house through the back door and saw the sheriff on the floor. They dashed out the front, but had no chance of locating Lyons in the dark. Jack Smith returned at once to Bill Withers, who said only, "Jack, I guess they have done me."

A messenger was sent immediately to the county seat at Eugene to inform Chief Deputy Fred Fisk of the shooting and to summon a doctor. Meanwhile, mortally wounded Sheriff Withers was taken by buggy to George Hale's stage house, where he was made as comfortable as possible until the physician could arrive from Eugene.

Back at the Lyons' house, Elliott's wife, mother, and father were placed under arrest for interfering with the sheriff. Constable Smith and Special Deputy Cornelius rounded up a few local residents as a posse and began searching for Lyons. By morning two large posses began scouring the Coast Range hills for Elliott Lyons, but the fugitive, familiar with the country, seemed to have disappeared.

On February 7, a day and a half after being shot, Bill Withers died at Hale's Stage House, his wife by his side.

All of western Oregon was in an uproar over the murder of the popular sheriff, and a reward of $1,500 was

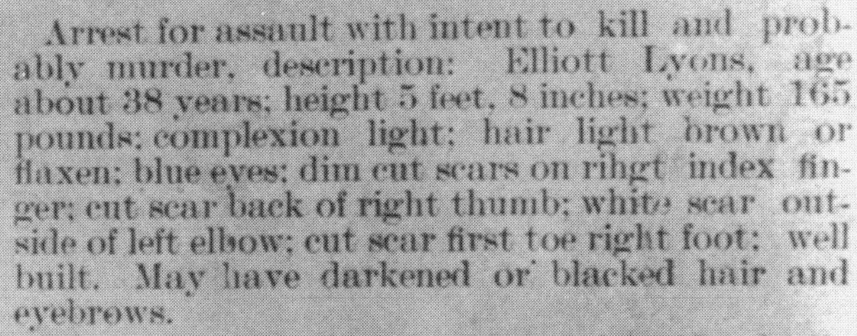

$500 REWARD.

Sheriff's Office, Eugene, Feb. 5, 1903.

Arrest for assault with intent to kill and probably murder, description: Elliott Lyons, age about 38 years; height 5 feet, 8 inches; weight 165 pounds; complexion light; hair light brown or flaxen; blue eyes; dim cut scars on rihgt index finger; cut scar back of right thumb; white scar outside of left elbow; cut scar first toe right foot; well built. May have darkened or blacked hair and eyebrows.

The above-described man shot and probably fatally wounded Sheriff W. W. Withers of Lane County, Oregon, on the evening of Feb. 5th, while the latter was endeavoring to arrest him on a warrant for horse stealing. I hold a warrant and want this man bad. Arrest and hold him and wire me. All information thankfully received.

FRED FISK, Deputy Sheriff, Lane Co., Oregon.

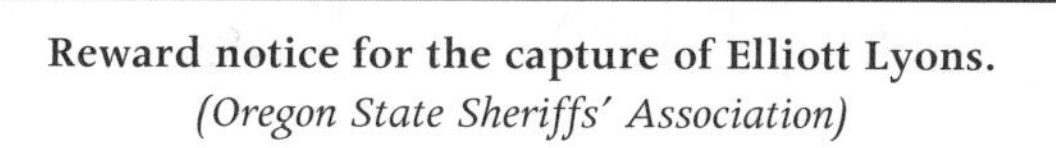

Reward notice for the capture of Elliott Lyons.

(Oregon State Sheriffs' Association)

posted for Lyons' capture. Lawmen and volunteers by the dozens searched carefully through the farm and hill country of Lane County.

On the morning of February 9, just after eight o'clock, a posse that had been patrolling the wagon road and railroad tracks at Creswell, twelve miles south of Eugene, spotted a man climbing into an empty boxcar of a train that was just pulling out of the station. The seven possemen rode quickly to the front of the train and motioned the engineer to stop. Then they approached the boxcar and took the man out at gunpoint. They had captured Elliott Lyons.

On the way to jail at Eugene, Lyons told his captors that on the night of the shooting he had already decided the first lawman who tried to draw a gun on him was going to get shot—Withers happened to be the man.

On February 10 the large black headlines of the *Eugene Morning Register* exclaimed: "WITHERS' MURDERER IS IN JAIL." That edition also carried a plea by Editor W.G. Gilstrap: "Everybody keep cool. Let there be no mob violence. Let Eugene be orderly. Our reputation as a city is at stake. Justice will be promptly meted out to Lyons, for the law will deal with him as he should be dealt with."

On April 17, 1903, the man who brazenly told jailers: "Any person attempting to get the drop on me does not value his life," made a drop of his own—from a scaffold in the yard behind the Lane County jail.

How City Marshal Jasper Westfall Died

The dusty small settlement of Westfall, forty-seven miles west of Ontario, Oregon, still retained its frontier image in 1912. False-fronted buildings stood beside the dirt main street, with small wood-frame houses scattered behind. Established in 1882 and named for the area's first

Westfall is now a wind-blown ghost town in the high desert country.
(Authors' 1990 photo)

settler, Levi Westfall, the town remained active as a trading and social center for ranchers and homesteaders in that remote sage and rimrock district of Malheur County well into this century.

May 10, 1912 was a warm, quiet Friday in Westfall. Not many people were in town since it was a work day for the ranch hands, who would not come in until Saturday night. Ben Corbett and Wayne Hyde were clerking in the main mercantile establishment, the Jones and Company store, while next door Lee Ridgeway was tending bar at the Hart Saloon. Across the street, Frank Jones was sweeping out his saloon, and next to him Joe Coburn's barber shop was open but having a slow day. Phil Pfifer's anvil was ringing in his blacksmith shop. The only other sound to break the quiet was an occasional shout of greeting from passersby. That is the peaceful kind of day it was in

Westfall on that Friday in May, but it was not the way the day would end.

Asa Carey was mad. He had been in the saloons drinking most of the day, watering a grudge he held against Mayor William West, City Marshal Jasper Westfall, and the town in general. Carey, thirty-three, had been the town terror for years. A bully and drunkard, the ex-blacksmith had shot Frank Cammann to death six years before in the Hart Saloon, and three years after that had beat young Dan Brady so unmercifully in a fight that he died a few days later. Most people were afraid of Asa Carey.

Because of his fearless demeanor and his ready fists, however, Carey had been the previous city marshal, a job requiring a man sturdy enough to control drunk, rowdy cowboys, and other assorted troublemakers. But there was

City Marshal Jasper Westfall.
(Malheur County Historical Society)

a problem: Carey had an increasing tendency to settle his own personal disputes with the weight of his badge. Therefore, on May 7, Mayor William West and other town leaders took the city marshal's star away from Carey and gave it to a man whom they knew to be sober, courageous, law-abiding, and most of all, fair: Jasper Westfall, a descendant of early settlers.

Asa Carey was infuriated at the action of the city fathers. For several days the more he stewed about it, the more he drank. He teamed up with a man named Art Ricketts to do some hard drinking on May 10, and that's when the trouble started. Carey and Ricketts were both armed with revolvers as they began their drinking in the town's two saloons. All day Carey boasted that he was the better man for the marshal's job, and that Jasper Westfall was not up to the task. As whiskey increased Carey's bravado, the abusive comments about Jasper and the mayor became louder and more frequent, to the point where the incensed ex-marshal started yelling in the street.

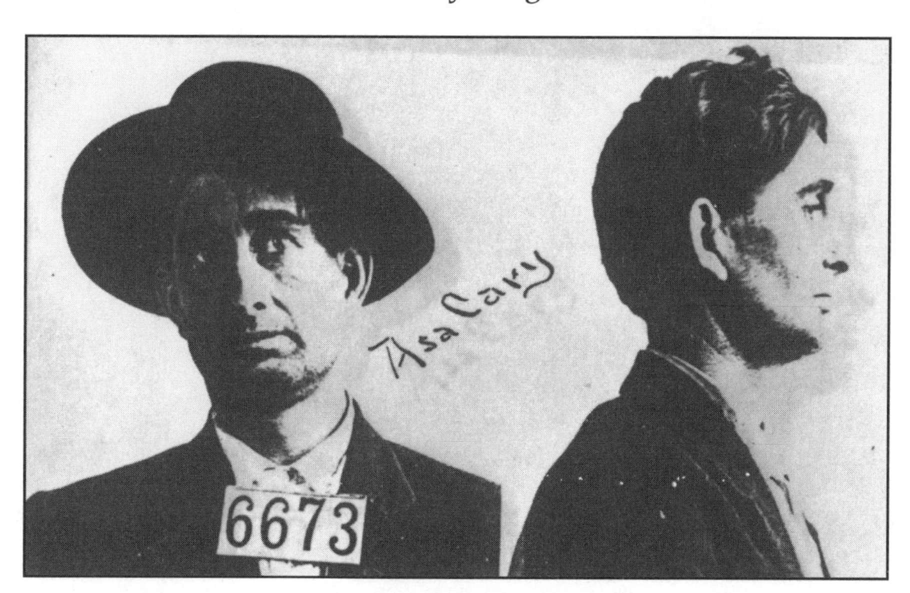

Asa Carey. *(Oregon State Archives)*

Carey and Ricketts then reentered the Jones Saloon, where they had a couple more drinks. Carey walked out onto the front porch. He began whooping and yelling that the new marshal should come and try to arrest him. Then he started shooting into the air and into the roof of the saloon porch.

Marshal Jasper Westfall was at his home, about a block northeast of the Jones Saloon. He heard the trouble Asa was causing and headed for the scene to quiet him down. As Jasper approached the saloon, he saw a number of townspeople watching the proceedings from places of cover. Ben Corbett and Wayne Hyde, the Jones and Company clerks, were standing out in front of the store about thirty feet across the street from Asa Carey, who was still in front of the saloon punctuating his shouts with gunshots into the air.

Unarmed, Jasper walked calmly up to Carey and told

Jasper Westfall's house still stands in 1990. *(Authors' photo)*

The Jones and Company store as it appeared in 1990. The Westfall-Carey gunfight took place at the right center of photo and the Hart Saloon stood in the open space in front of the trees. *(Authors' photo)*

him he was to quiet down immediately. Carey stared at Jasper and said that if Westfall tried to arrest him, he would kill him on the spot. Carey then spewed an abusive string of oaths at the new marshal. Again Jasper warned Asa Carey to leave and go home or be arrested, but his words had no effect.

To the continued shouts of abuse and threats by Carey, Westfall turned and walked back toward his house. There he buckled on his Colt revolver and strode briskly back to the main street. Carey was now standing in front of the Hart Saloon, next to the Jones and Company store. From doors and windows, the frightened townspeople were watching.

With his gun holstered, the marshal walked to within ten feet of Asa Carey and told him he was under arrest.

Carey, who had put his gun into his pocket, backed up a few steps. When Jasper ordered Asa to come with him, Carey quickly pulled his gun and Westfall pulled his. It was never positively determined from the witnesses which man shot first. The marshal fired once and missed. Carey shot three times, two of the bullets hitting Westfall.

Jasper fell to the ground and Carey swung his gun around at the others, asking if anyone else wanted trouble with him. He then stooped over the dying man and snatched up the marshal's revolver. A moment later he stepped into the Hart Saloon, put Jasper's gun on the bar in front of Lee Ridgeway, and asked for a drink. Ben Corbett came in to calm him down, as he had tried to be on friendly terms with Carey in the past. Ben told Carey that he should turn over the other gun, too, as there had been enough shooting.

The Hart Saloon where Marshal Westfall died.
(Malheur County Historical Society)

Carey pointed his revolver at Corbett and at Jack Fairman, who had entered with Ben, and said he was not going to turn over his gun and that if Corbett was his friend, he would go get him some more cartridges from the Jones and Company store next door. Corbett agreed, playing along, and asked Carey to come with him.

The unsuspecting killer followed Ben out of the saloon. Upon reaching the door of the store, Corbett fell back to let Carey enter first. As Carey walked through the doorway, Corbett jumped him and pinned his arms to his sides. Jack Fairman and another man helped hold Carey until he could be securely trussed.

Meanwhile, Jasper Westfall was carried into the Hart Saloon, where he was laid on a billiard table. Dr. Henry Schenk was summoned, but there was no hope for the wounded marshal. Within forty-five minutes, with his wife Daisy by his side, he died.

The captured gunman was taken up the street to the tiny one-cell, rock-walled jail and locked in leg-irons and handcuffs before the door was bolted. Later that evening, Malheur County Deputy Sheriff Ben Brown arrived by buggy from his office. Amid threats of lynching by the angry townsfolk, he transported Carey about thirty miles to the county jail at Vale.

The funeral of City Marshal Jasper Westfall was the largest ever held in the town. Thirty-six buggies and wagons and hundreds of people proceeded out to the tiny cemetery in the sage flats to say goodbye.

As for Asa Carey, he was convicted of murder and sent to the state penitentiary at Salem under a life sentence. He was later paroled and moved to Napa, California.

The Westfall city jail, as it appeared in 1990, where Carey was held after the killing. *(Authors' photo)*

Sheriff Til Taylor, Umatilla County

Til Taylor, the remarkable sheriff of Umatilla County, was the most widely known of any Oregon lawman killed in the line of duty. He had been sheriff for eighteen years when he was murdered on the afternoon of July 25, 1920. The Pendleton *East Oregonian* said of him shortly after his death: "He was a competent, dependable, fearless officer and at the same time had a personal charm and sincerity of manner that won enduring friendships...On countless occasions his skill and daring stood between the peace of this county and the acts of lawless men. We grew so accustomed to hearing of successful exploits by our sheriff that the news became commonplace."

His full name was Tilman D. Taylor, and he grew up on a farm near Athena, fifteen miles northeast of Pendleton.

Tilman D. Taylor, Umatilla County Sheriff, 1902–1920.
(Oregon State Sheriffs' Association)

Sheriff Til Taylor was a favorite figure in the annual Pendleton Roundup parade.
(Oregon State Sheriffs' Association)

After years in the hardware business, Til opted for a career as a lawman. In 1898, at thirty-two years of age, he was appointed deputy sheriff for Umatilla County. He was a natural law officer; firm when he had to be, pleasant when he could be, Til quickly proved his worth. In those days Umatilla County was rugged and rough, gambling houses and saloons ran wide-open day and night, and it took a good eye and a keen mind to stay one jump ahead of the lawbreakers.

Deputy Taylor served four years under Sheriff William Blakely, brother of James Blakely, the Prineville lawman who had routed the vigilantes. When William Blakely retired in 1902, he urged Til to run for sheriff, and the popular deputy was elected.

It was Til's policy never to shoot a man when it was

possible to bring him in alive, and only one time did he find it necessary to shoot at someone. He was on the trail of two bank robbers from Hermiston. He tracked and found both men on the Umatilla River near the Columbia. While holding one struggling prisoner, he fought a gun battle with the other outlaw. After several shots Til's gun jammed and the second bandit got away. Til traced the man through three states, finally arresting him in Montana.

Sheriff Taylor repeatedly set out alone to chase down and arrest lawbreakers, returning with them alive. Included in those occasions were twenty-six of the twenty-eight men who broke out of jail over the years. In his career, Til Taylor made 2,645 arrests without ever killing a man.

On Sunday, July 25, 1920, the sheriff had some work to clear up in the office. After working for some time, he

The Umatilla County courthouse in Pendleton, where Sheriff Til Taylor was killed in his second- floor office on July 25, 1920.
(Oregon State Sheriffs' Association)

went out to an early-afternoon supper with a friend, Guy Wyrick. While Til was gone, Deputy Jacob Martin was taken by surprise in the jail and slugged as he brought food into the cells for the prisoners. Soon, Jack Rathie, a thief, and Jim Owens and Neil Hart, armed robbers whom Til had arrested ten days earlier, were on the loose in the courthouse building, which housed the jail and sheriff's office.

As the three escapees were ransacking Til's office, collecting guns and looking for ammunition, the sheriff and Wyrick strolled in, unaware of what had happened. They ran smack into the prisoners. Til began grappling with Owens, and Wyrick jumped on Rathie. The fight was short but furious. Til's revolver fell from its holster. Hart leaped for the gun. He pointed it at Til, who was now on the floor with Owens. The lawman freed one hand long

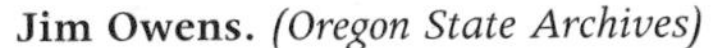

Jim Owens. *(Oregon State Archives)*

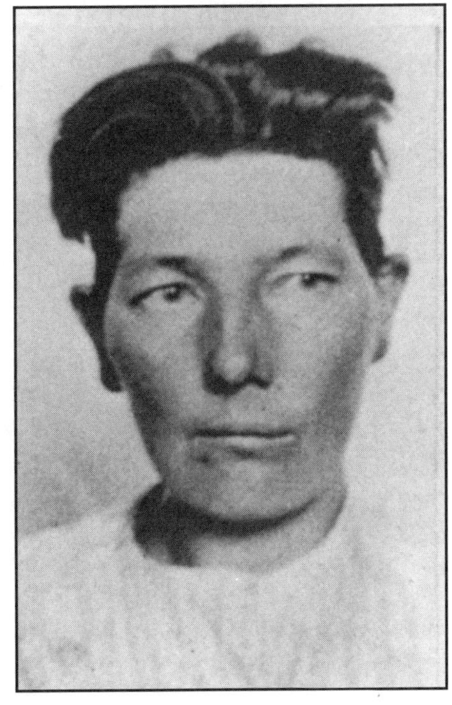

Neil Hart. *(Oregon State Archives)*

enough to grab Hart's gun hand. The gun went off, sending a bullet into the wall. Hart jerked his hand away from Til's grasp and shot the sheriff in the neck, the bullet ripping down into his chest. Then the three outlaws escaped from the building.

Guy Wyrick gave the alarm that Til Taylor had been shot during a jailbreak. The dying sheriff was taken to St. Anthony's Hospital where he lasted only a few hours, succumbing at 6 p.m.

The people of Pendleton were stunned. They went into action to find Til Taylor's killers. A full-scale manhunt was soon underway, assisted by lawmen from Union County, Morrow County, Portland, and Walla Walla. Even the Oregon-Washington Railway & Navigation Company sent three special agents to help in the search. Hundreds of Umatilla County townspeople, ranchers, and farmers joined the hunt as well. A $6,000 dead-or-alive reward was posted by Til's brother, W.R. Taylor, known as Jinks. Jinks was immediately appointed sheriff to complete Til's term.

With no clue to the direction the fleeing outlaws had taken, posses scouted the countryside, searching fields, hills, and creek bottoms. Bloodhounds were brought down from the prison at Walla Walla. But one sighting after another proved false.

After six days and nights of effort, possemen under Union County Deputy J.P. McLaughlin and Malheur County Deputy Lee Noe looked into a sheep camp tent at Spout Springs in the Blue Mountains southeast of Pendleton. There, in the early morning darkness, the lawmen found the sleeping forms of Neil Hart and Jim Owens. The fugitives were well-armed. Hart was supposed to have stood guard, but exhaustion had driven him to sleep.

Jack Rathie, the other member of the outlaw trio, was

taken the next day sixteen miles to the west when he stopped at a cabin asking for breakfast. The manhunt had ended much less dramatically than it had begun, and it carried on Til Taylor's tradition of capture without killing.

Capital punishment had been reinstated in Oregon a month prior to Til Taylor's death. Hart, Owens, and Rathie were all convicted of first-degree murder, though only Neil Hart actually pulled the trigger. All three were hanged at the state penitentiary. When the last man dropped, Jinks Taylor, who witnessed the executions, wired the editor of the Pendleton *East Oregonian:* "The untimely death of Tilman Taylor has been avenged."

Sheriff Austin Goodman, Harney County

In the summer of 1924, Sheriff Austin Goodman was thinking of retiring as a lawman. Though only fifty-four years old, for ten years he had served as sheriff of a county so large that its 10,228 square miles dwarfed some states. He was constantly on the go through his massive district on the vast sage plains of eastern Oregon, some trips taking him 150 miles south to the California border. He longed to have more time with his wife and three children at home in Burns. Since his term would be finished in January, Austin reckoned it would be a good time to retire. But until then he intended to do his job.

On the morning of August 27, 1924, after an exhausting trip to Denio, down on the Nevada line, Austin stopped to rest awhile at the Juniper Ranch in the shadow of Steens Mountain, about seventy miles southeast of Burns. Ranch manager Harold Cawlfield told the sheriff that a man named Arch Cody had given him a worthless bank draft, and said Cody could likely be found down the road at the Pollack ranch.

Harney County Sheriff William Austin Goodman. *(Oregon State Sheriffs' Association)*

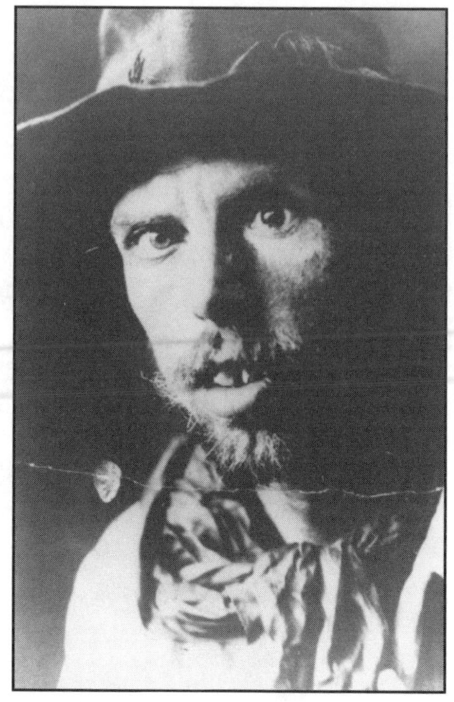

Outlaw Arch Cody was hanged for the murder of Sheriff Goodman. *(Oregon State Sheriffs' Association)*

Cody, forty-four, was an old-style outlaw, a horse thief who had spent three years in prison. He was presently wanted in California, though how much of his past Goodman knew is not clear. The sheriff proceeded to the C.L. Pollack place, just over the line in Malheur County, and there he found Arch Cody. Goodman told Cody he was under arrest. The outlaw offered no resistance at the time, but asked the sheriff if he could attend to his horse. Sheriff Goodman agreed and did not follow him to the corral.

When Cody reached his horse, he took his .30-30 Winchester from the saddle scabbard and turned back toward the lawman. Goodman warned him to put down the rifle. When Cody made no move to do so, the sheriff said that two could play at that game and reached for his own gun. Cody fired. Austin Goodman staggered, pitching forward on the ground. Cody then mounted his horse and galloped away.

Sheriff Goodman died within the hour, after telling those who ran to help him that he believed he was finished. The next day his body was taken to Burns.

The hunt was on for Arch Cody. As soon as it could be arranged, men were sent out on horseback to scour every inch of the area. It was a job willingly accepted by Harney County ranchers and cowhands, as Sheriff Goodman had made many friends in the lonely sage country. By the next morning, posses headed by Sheriff Lee Noe of Malheur County, Sheriff Ole H. Olson of Crook County, and Sheriff Cy Bingham of Grant County spread through the rangelands of the Harney and Malheur country.

The lawmen learned the outlaw had spent the night in a sheep pasture near John Jenkin's ranch and that same morning had gone up into nearby Stone House Canyon. Possemen rode for the canyon and upon reaching it separated into two groups, each working along opposite sides of the hill.

Suddenly, Cody was spotted riding hard near the head of the canyon. Shots were fired at him with no effect. Soon the killer was in full view, spurring his exhausted horse in a last dash for freedom. He began shooting at the posse, and a running gun fight ensued between lawmen and the desperate outlaw.

Upon reaching the brow of the hill, Cody saw more men riding toward him, led by rancher Roy Skeins. Skeins and his riders began shooting at Cody from in front, and the posse, firing from below, was quickly closing the gap. Throwing down his rifle, Cody rolled off his winded horse and raised his hands. The chase was over.

When the possemen reached the outlaw, who had been

unscathed by the fusillade of bullets, they found that in addition to the Winchester rifle, he had been armed with two .32-caliber revolvers and a large knife. Arch Cody was tried and convicted of first-degree murder. He was hanged at Salem in April 1925.

Funeral services for Austin Goodman were held on the lawn in front of the Burns courthouse. The crowd was said to be the largest ever to attend such services in the history of Harney County.

A Final Word . . .

By the mid-1920s, the era of old-time, six-gun outlaws and horseback lawmen was over, except for isolated incidents. Oregon had joined the march toward twentieth-century technology and modern law enforcement methods. The Matt Bledsoes, Ferd Pattersons, and Boone Helms of those long-gone days would find their lawless careers cut short by today's well-trained and equipped law officers, and Old Bill Miner would find to his disgust that modern trains carry no registered mail or express, and certainly no gold.

Oregon's history has surely included its share of desperadoes, but we should remember, as we read their stories from the safe distance of our armchairs, not to regard them as folk heroes. They were, after all, the scourge and terror of bygone days. Though we may be tempted to consider some of their exploits colorful and exciting, their passing was not mourned.

NOTES ON SOURCES

IN A BOOK OF THIS KIND, intended for the general reader, to footnote the exact and detailed record of every source examined is unnecessary. At the same time, we want to indicate the nature of the material to help those interested in pursuing any of the subjects further. Therefore, we have included a listing of the sources that comprised our research materials.

There have been no previous books featuring a wide collection of Oregon outlaw stories, though several good ones have chronicled one figure or incident or gang. In addition, articles in Western history magazines and general periodicals have profiled certain Pacific Northwest bandits.

Our chief reliance, however, was on primary records sources, such as penitentiary, jail, and court records, as well as contemporary newspapers. We examined hundreds of microfilmed editions of forty-five different newspapers, a pleasant task of time-travel at which we spent over 400 hours.

Diaries, journals, and "books of remembrances" were also helpful in our outlaw research, as they contained recollections of old-timers who were on the scene.

The photographs were gathered from a variety of

sources, including private collections, photo archives of historical societies and museums, as well as the authors' own collection. A number of lawmen's and other photos were provided through the courtesy of the Oregon State Sheriffs' Association, as noted in the credit lines.

SUGGESTIONS FOR FURTHER READING

Books on any of Oregon's outlaws are few, but for readers interested in exploring in greater depth these are highly recommended:

All For Nothing, by Larry Sturholm, gives the detailed account of the DeAutremont train holdup at Tunnel 13.

Black Bart, by Bill Collins and Bruce Levene, offers a close look at Wells, Fargo's chief nemesis, including his forays into Oregon.

Last of the Bandit Riders, by Matt Warner, is good for information on the McCarty Gang in Oregon.

The Murder of Til Taylor, by Ernest Crockatt, is an excellent chronicle by one who knew Sheriff Taylor.

Sources

Books

Baker County Historical Society. *Baker City Centennial Album*. Baker City, Oregon: Baker County Historical Society, 1974.

Bancroft, H.H. *Popular Tribunals - Vol. I*. San Francisco: The History Company, Publishers, 1887.

Blankenship, Russell. *And There Were Men*. New York: Alfred A. Knopf, 1942.

Boessenecker, John. *Badge and Buckshot: Lawlessness in Old California*. Norman, Oklahoma: University of Oklahoma Press, 1988.

Brimlow, George F. *Harney County, Oregon and Its Rangeland*. Burns, Oregon: Harney County Historical Society, 1980.

Brogan, Phil F. *East of the Cascades*. Portland, Oregon: Binfords & Mort, Publishers, 1964.

Burrell, O.K. *Gold in the Woodpile: An Informal History of Banking in Oregon*. Eugene, Oregon: University of Oregon Books, 1967.

Carey, Charles H. *A General History of Oregon*. Portland, Oregon: Binfords & Mort, Publishers, 1922.

Clark, Robert C. *History of Willamette Valley, Oregon*. Three vols. Chicago: S.J. Clarke Publishing Co., 1927.

Coffman, Lloyd W. *Pioneering in the Wallowa*. Enterprise, Oregon: Wallowa County Centennial Press, 1987.

Collins, William and Levene, Bruce. *Black Bart*. Mendocino, California: Pacific Transcriptions, 1992.

Crockatt, Ernest L. *The Murder of Til Taylor*. Philadelphia, Pennsylvania: Dorrance & Company, 1970.

Crook County Historical Society. *History of Crook County*. Prineville, Oregon: Crook County Historical Society, 1981.

DeNevi, Donald P. *Western Train Robberies*. Millbrae, California: Celestial Arts, 1976.

Dillon, Richard. *Wells, Fargo Detective*. New York: Coward-McCann, 1969.

Dimsdale, Thomas J. *The Vigilantes of Montana*. Norman, Oklahoma: University of Oklahoma Press, 1953.

Dodge, Orvil. *Pioneer History of Coos & Curry Counties, Oregon*. Salem, Oregon: Capital Printing Co., 1898.

Fagan, David D. *History of Benton County, Oregon*. Portland, Oregon: Walling Co., 1885.

Friedman, Ralph. *Tracking Down Oregon*. Caldwell, Idaho: The Caxton Printers, 1978.

Furlong, Charles W. *Let 'Er Buck*. New York: G.P. Putnam & Sons, 1921.

Gilliam County Historical Society. *History of Gilliam County*. Condon, Oregon: Gilliam County Historical Society, 1981.

Glasscock, C.B. *Bandits and the Southern Pacific*. New York: Stokes & Company, 1929.

Good, Rachael Applegate. *History of Klamath County, Oregon*. Klamath Falls, Oregon: privately published, 1941.

Gregg, Jacob R. *Pioneer Days in Malheur County*. Los Angeles: privately published, 1950.

Haines, Francis D. *Jacksonville: A Biography of a Gold Camp*. Medford, Oregon: privately published, 1967.

Hiatt, Isaac. *Thirty-one Years in Baker County*. Baker City, Oregon: privately published, 1893.

Hill, Edna May. *Josephine County Historical Highlights, Vols. I and II*. Grants Pass, Oregon: Josephine County Historical Society, 1976 and 1979.

Horan, James D. *Desperate Men*. Garden City, New York: Doubleday & Company, 1962.

__________ . *The Pinkertons*. New York: Crown Publishers, Inc., 1967.

__________ . *The Wild Bunch*. New York: Signet, 1958.

Hough, Emerson. *The Story of the Outlaw: A Study of the Western Desperado*. New York: Grosset & Dunlap, 1905.

Hungerford, Edward. *Wells Fargo: Advancing the American Frontier*. New York: Bonanza Books, 1949.

Juris, Frances. *Old Crook County*. Prineville, Oregon: privately published, 1975.

Kelly, Charles. *The Outlaw Trail*. New York: Bonanza Books, 1958.

Kelly, Joseph "Bunco." *Thirteen Years in Oregon State Penitentiary*. Portland: privately published, 1909.

King, E.L. and Mahaffey, R.E. *Main Line: Fifty Years of Railroading with the Southern Pacific*. Garden City, New York: Doubleday & Company, 1948.

Klamath County Historical Society. *History of Klamath County, Oregon*. Klamath Falls, Oregon, 1984.

Langford, Nathanial P. *Vigilante Days and Ways*. New York: D.D. Merrill & Company, 1893.

Lockley, Fred. *Oregon Folks*. New York: The Knickerbocker Press, 1927.

Macnab, Gordon. *A Century of News and People in the East Oregonian*. Pendleton, Oregon: East Oregonian Publishing Company, 1975.

McArthur, Lewis A. *Oregon Geographical Names*. Portland: Western Imprints (Oregon Historical Society), 1982.
McConnell, W.J. *Early History of Idaho*. Caldwell, Idaho: The Caxton Printers, 1913.
McKeown, Martha. *The Trail Led North*. New York: Macmillan,1948.
Meier, Gary and Gloria. *Knights of the Whip: Stagecoach Days in Oregon*. Bellevue, Washington: Timeline Publishing Company, 1987.
Moore, Lucia W. *The Story of Eugene*. New York: Stratford House, 1949.
Morn, Frank. *The Eye That Never Sleeps*. Bloomington,Indiana: Indiana University Press, 1982.
Parson, Colonel William. *History of Umatilla and Morrow Counties, Oregon*. Chicago: W.H. Lever Company, 1902.
Patterson, Richard. *Train Robbery*. Boulder, Colorado: Johnson Books, 1981.
Pointer, Larry. *In Search of Butch Cassidy*. Norman, Oklahoma: University of Oklahoma Press, 1977.
Potter, Miles F. *Oregon's Golden Years*. Caldwell, Idaho: The Caxton Printers, 1976.
Prassel, Frank R. *The Western Peace Officer*. Norman, Oklahoma: University of Oklahoma Press, 1972.
"Prisoner No. 5235." *A Sketch of the Oregon State Penitentiary*. Salem, Oregon: Oregon State Penitentiary, 1908.
"Prisoner No. 6435." *The Oregon Penitentiary*. Salem, Oregon: Oregon State Penitentiary, 1917.
"Prisoner No. 6435." *Sensational Prison Escapes*. Salem, Oregon: Oregon State Penitentiary, 1922.
Scott, Harvey W. *History of the Oregon Country, six vols*. Cambridge, Massachusetts: Riverside Press, 1924.
Searcy, Mildred. *We Remember*. Pendleton, Oregon: East Oregonian Publishing Company, 1973.
Shaver, E.F. *History of Central Oregon*. Spokane, Washington: Western Historical Publishing Company, 1905.
Smith, Earl. *The Westfall Country*. New York: Exposition Press, 1963.
Steber, Rick. *Union Centennial Album*. Union, Oregon: Union Centennial Productions, 1978.
Steeves, Sarah H. *Book of Remembrances of Marion County Pioneers*. Portland, Oregon: The Berncliff Press, 1927.
Stewart, D.J. *History of Siskiyou County, California*. Oakland, California: Stewart Company, 1881.
Sturholm, Larry and Howard, John. *All For Nothing: The True Story of the Last Great American Train Robbery*. Portland, Oregon: BLS Publishing Company, 1976.
Swallow, Alan. *The Wild Bunch*. Denver, Colorado: privately published, 1966.
Walling, A.G. *History of Lane County, Oregon*. Portland, Oregon: Walling & Company, 1884.

_________ . *History of Southern Oregon*. Portland, Oregon: Walling & Company, 1884.

Warner, Matt. *Last of the Bandit Riders*. New York: Bonanza, 1938.

Western Historical Publishing Company. *Illustrated History of Baker, Grant, Malheur, and Harney Counties, Oregon*. Chicago: Western Historical Publishing Company, 1902.

_________ . *Illustrated History of Union and Wallowa Counties, Oregon*. Chicago: Western Historical Publishing Company, 1902.

Winther, Oscar O. *The Great Northwest*. New York: Alfred A. Knopf, 1948.

PERIODICALS

Braly, David. "Central Oregon Dictator," *Cascades East*, Fall 1987.

Branigar, Thomas. "The Murder of Cyrenius C. Hooker," *Oregon Historical Quarterly*, Vol. LXXV, No. 4, December 1974.

Bright, Verne. "Sailors Diggings in the Siskiyous," *Western Folklore*, July 1952.

Carey, Elton. "Reign of the Vigilantes," *Frontier Times*, December-January 1970.

Dullenty, James. "Bad Blood–The True Story of Harry Tracy," *Old West*, Summer 1983.

Fishnell, David. "The McCarty Gang & The Delta Holdup," *Old West*, Spring 1985.

Henderson, Grace G. "The McCarty Gang in Oregon," *Old West*, Summer 1977.

Manring, B.F. "Recollections of a Pioneer of 1859, Lawson Stockman," *Oregon Historical Quarterly*, Vol. II, June 1900.

Nedry, H.S. "Early History of Grant County," *Oregon Historical Quarterly*, December 1952.

Noll, Lowell. "South Idaho Vigilantism, *Pacific Northwesterner*, Vol. 2, No. 2, Spring 1958.

Pfeifer, William. "Men Who Wore the Oregon Boot," *Old West*, Winter 1966.

Rickards, Colin. "Boone Helm--Man Eater!", *True West*, March-April 1973.

Stewart, Patricia. "They Knew the McCartys," *The West*, August 1967.

Stoner, Mary E. "My Father Was a Train Robber," *True West*, August 1983.

Tracy, Charles A. "Police Function in Portland, 1851–1874," *Oregon Historical Quarterly*, Spring, Summer, Fall 1979.

Tucker, Gerald J. "Hank Vaughn's Fatal Ride," *Frontier Times*, April-May 1966.

Turner, William M. "Pioneer Justice in Oregon," *Overland Monthly*, March 1874.

Warren, Larry. "Oregon's Legendary Sheriff," *Frontier Times*, October-November 1973.

White, Magner. "Dave Tucker," *American Magazine*, September 1929.

Winton, Harry N.M., ed. "The Powder River and John Day Mines in 1862: Diary of Winfield Scott Ebey," *Pacific Northwest Quarterly*, October 1942.

Newspapers

Advertiser, Brownsville, Oregon.
Albany Democrat-Herald, Albany, Oregon.
Alta California, San Francisco, California.
Ashland Tidings, Ashland, Oregon.
Athena Press, Athena, Oregon.
Bedrock Democrat, Baker City, Oregon.
Blue Mountain American, Sumpter, Oregon.
Blue Mountain Eagle, Canyon City, Oregon.
Burns Times-Herald, Burns, Oregon.
Chief Joseph Herald, Joseph, Oregon.
Chronicle, San Francisco, California.
Coos Bay Times, Marshfield, Oregon.
Daily Courier, Grants Pass, Oregon.
Democratic Times, Jacksonville, Oregon.
Douglas Independent, Roseburg, Oregon.
East Oregonian, Pendleton, Oregon.
Ensign, Roseburg, Oregon.
Eugene Guard, Eugene, Oregon.
Eugene Morning Register, Eugene, Oregon.
Eugene Register, Eugene, Oregon.
Eugene Register-Guard, Eugene, Oregon.
Gazette-Times, Corvallis, Oregon.
La Grande Gazette, La Grande, Oregon.
Malheur Enterprise, Vale, Oregon.
Mediator, Portland, Oregon.
Mountaineer, The Dalles, Oregon.
Ontario Democrat, Ontario, Oregon.
Oregonian, Portland, Oregon.
Oregon Journal, Portland, Oregon.
Oregon Sentinel, Jacksonville, Oregon.
Oregon Statesman, Salem, Oregon.
Pendleton Tribune, Pendleton, Oregon.
Plaindealer, Roseburg, Oregon.
Record-Chieftain, Enterprise, Oregon.
Roseburg News-Review, Roseburg, Oregon.
St. Helens Sentinel-Mist, St. Helens, Oregon.
Umpqua Ensign, Roseburg, Oregon.
Vancouver Independent, Vancouver, Washington.
Wallowa County Chieftain, Enterprise, Oregon.
Wallowa Herald, Joseph, Oregon.
Weekly Mountaineer, The Dalles, Oregon.
Weekly Oregonian, Portland, Oregon.
Yamhill County Reporter, McMinnville, Oregon.
Yreka Journal, Yreka, California.

ARCHIVES AND RECORDS

Oregon Bankers' Association. Records. 1891–1935.

Oregon State Archives. Penitentiary records and annual reports. 1859–1920.

Oregon State Sheriffs' Association. Miscellaneous records, reports, and memorabilia.

Oregon Territorial Supreme Court. Case of Territory of Oregon v. Nimrod O'Kelley. 1 Oregon Reports 51. December 1851.

Pinkerton's, Inc. Archives. Research Typescript on Bill Miner. Undated.

Sheriff's records. Baker County. Baker City, Oregon.

Sheriff's records. Clackamus County. Oregon City, Oregon.

Sheriff's records. Harney County. Burns, Oregon.

Sheriff's records. Lane County. Eugene, Oregon.

Sheriff's records. Malheur County. Vale, Oregon.

Sheriff's records. Multnomah County. Portland, Oregon.

Sheriff's records. Polk County. Dallas, Oregon.

Sheriff's records. Umatilla County. Pendleton, Oregon.

Sheriff's records. Wasco County. The Dalles, Oregon.

Wells Fargo records. J.B. Hume scrapbooks, 1873–1904; *Robbers' Record,* 1885; Miscellaneous company records. Wells Fargo Bank History Department, San Francisco, California.

MANUSCRIPTS AND MISCELLANEOUS DOCUMENTS

Adams, Row W. "The Oregon Style." Unpublished M.A. Thesis, University of Oregon, Eugene, Oregon, 1958.

Edwards, Mrs. Charles S. "Central Oregon History Scrapbooks." Oregon Historical Society Library, Portland, Oregon, undated.

Index

The authors welcome comments and suggestions for subsequent editions of *Oregon Outlaws, Tales of Old-Time Desperadoes*. Please write c/o Tamarack Books, PO Box 190313, Boise, ID 83719-0313.

Additional copies of *Oregon Outlaws, Tales of Old-Time Desperadoes* can be found in fine bookstores nationwide or directly from the publisher.

If ordering direct, please include a check for $20.95 (book @ $17.95 plus a shipping/handling charge of $3.00). Idaho residents should send $21.85 (book @ $17.95, shipping/handling $3.00, and Idaho tax $.90).

Send your name, address, and check to:

Oregon Outlaws, Tales of Old-Time Desperadoes Orders
Tamarack Books, Inc.
PO Box 190313
Boise, ID 83719-0313

To place orders using MasterCard or Visa,
Please call 1-800-962-6657.

For information on other Tamarack titles
please call 1-800-962-6657.

Ask for our free catalog!